# Does God Exist?

## CARL LOFMARK

## RATIONALIST PRESS ASSOCIATION

London 1990

*Does God Exist?*

First published in August 1990

© Carl Lofmark and the Rationalist Press Association 1990

ISBN 0 301 90002 7

Published by the Rationalist Press Association
88 Islington High Street
London N1 8EW
England

Printed by R.A.P. Ltd.
201 Spotland Road·
Rochdale OL12 7AF
England

# Does God Exist?

*Concerning the gods, I cannot say that they exist nor yet that they do not exist. There are more reasons than one why we cannot know. There is the obscurity of the subject and the brevity of human life.*

Protagoras (about 500 BC)

# Does God Exist?

It is said that the French mathematician Laplace presented to the emperor Napoleon a copy of his famous book on the motions of the heavenly bodies. Napoleon asked him what was the place of God in his system. To this Laplace replied: "I have no need of that hypothesis."

The hypothesis of God is one of very many which people have used in the course of their history to explain to themselves the workings of the world around them. Since the dawn of civilisation, and probably long before, nature's processes have been accounted for with the help of a great variety of gods, together with a host of devils and demons, angels and cherubim, elves and fairies, ghosts and spirits good and evil. In the hope that such beings would use their powers to grant them life or victory or rain and a good harvest, people have flattered them with worship and appeased them with sacrifices. (The history of religion has been mischievously described as man's attempt to communicate with the weather.)

For thousands of years diseases were understood as the action of malignant spirits which invade the body and need to be exorcised; up to our own time calamities have been popularly attributed to sorcery and witchcraft. At the birth of modern physics the great astronomer Kepler supposed it was angels that kept the planets on their proper paths, while Newton required a God to wind up the clockwork of his great celestial machine. The more educated among the ancient Greeks believed in one God who animated the cosmos, while the not so educated feared and worshipped a whole pantheon of gods and spirits who, they believed, were constantly interfering in human affairs. The position was not much different in Christian Britain a couple of centuries ago, when people believed not only in God, but in the Devil as well as numerous angels, ghosts and spirits.

1

Of all these supposed but unseen beings very few now remain, at least in our Western society. With the advance of science, new hypotheses were found which explained the workings of nature more clearly and consistently, and so these supernatural beings lost their place in our picture of the world. For the last two or three generations most of them have become incredible, if not ridiculous, despite some lingering popular superstitions about ghosts and fairies.

Out of the multitude of spiritual powers that once directed the course of nature, only one survives. God has proved hardier than all his kind, and still today he occupies a very great place in the beliefs and practices and in the hopes and fears of all nations. Millions of people, most of whom reject in general all ideas of magic and the supernatural, continue to believe in God. As in centuries gone by, they meet to worship and pray to him, and their feelings about him are so strong that many of them will freely dedicate their lives to his service, and sometimes risk life itself for his sake.

Because that belief is so widely held and plays so important a part in our world today, most of us must have asked ourselves, at some time or other, whether or not God really exists. Those who decide that he does are apt to draw conclusions which may radically affect their other beliefs and opinions and alter the way they live their lives.

When believers consider where they should stand on social questions, and especially on questions of right and wrong, they usually make up their minds in the light of the moral teachings of their religion which were laid down by God, while rationalists and humanists, who do not believe, try to consider what the likely consequences of each course of action will be and what will be best for the people concerned.

Often the result is the same. God commands, 'Thou shalt not steal', and humanists, too, are against stealing. But they disapprove for different reasons: the believer because God says it is wrong, the non-believer because the consequences are usually unpleasant. The believer tries to obey God, the humanist tries to avoid hurting people.

Unfortunately, their different approaches do not always lead to the same result. Most Christian and Jewish believers are against euthanasia because God commanded, 'Thou shalt not kill'. It makes no difference how desperately the sick man wants to die, because suicide, too, is against God's law. But humanists very often take the opposite view, that it is an act of unselfish love to give a painless death to someone who is suffering from an incurable disease.

The great majority of Christians, Jews, Muslims and Hindus are also opposed to contraception (though some of the churches have relaxed their opposition during the present century); but non-believers regard over-population as a major international problem that causes poverty and war and now threatens our world with ecological disaster.

Similarly with abortion: Christians believe 'Thou shalt not kill' and argue over whether or not the unborn child is really a person to whom that law applies, while non-believers care more about the health and the personal rights of the woman concerned.

Christian leaders are generally opposed to Sunday trading (except in cathedral bookshops), while Jews and Muslims still insist on the ritual slaughter of their meat while the animal is still fully conscious; non-believers usually find Sunday trading harmless but ritual slaughter disgusting. On these and on many other issues those people who form their opinions by trying to obey God reach different conclusions from those who consider only what is best for human beings (and other sentient animals).

People who believe God exists also believe that he laid down absolute standards of right and wrong which tell us how we ought to behave. Because they believe in those standards, they try to impose them on society, and because religions are organised and influential, they often succeed. That is why, for example, ritual slaughter is legal and regularly practised, while it is illegal to end a dying man's suffering by painless euthanasia.

3

On questions like these the way we see things is very likely to be affected by our belief or disbelief in a God who is the source of right and wrong. It is therefore important, for our social and moral behaviour as well as for our understanding of the world around us, that we should ask the fundamental religious question: Does God exist?

*             *             *

The word 'God' means different things to different people. The Christian may think of God as a loving Father, for the Pantheist he is a cosmic force that is active in nature, for the Hindu or Sikh he is a universal spirit; an ancient Egyptian might think of him as a sun disc or an anthropoid figure with a jackal's head, tribesmen might mean a local totem or the ancestor of the tribe. Some people believe God is an invisible spirit; others have thought he was a superhuman warrior. The Romans sometimes declared that their Caesar was a god. For Aristotle God was the Unmoved Mover at the heart of the cosmos, for Paul Tillich he is the "Ground of our Being", for Matthew Arnold "a power not ourselves that makes for righteousness". The *Catholic Encyclopaedia* defines him as "the one Supreme and Infinite Personal Being, the Creator and Ruler of the universe, to whom man owes obedience and worship".

Hundreds of millions of people say that God exists. On that point, it would seem, they are all in agreement. But if what they mean by 'God' is not the same, then that agreement is an illusion. The 'God' that one group accepts is not believed in by other groups. Those hundreds of millions may *say* the same thing when they claim that God exists, but since their word 'God' does not *mean* the same thing, they are not really in agreement.

Some say there is a common denominator: a single God about whom the various religions have different beliefs. But that does not solve the problem at all. If people believe different things about him - some say he is a person, and male, others that

4

he is a cosmic force and sexless; some say he is loving and good, while others do not; some say he is purely celestial while others think he is human or superhuman or partly human - then the God they believe in is not the same God, and their beliefs will contradict each other.

God, some say, sent Jesus to establish the Christian Church; others say he sent Muhammad to establish Islam. Those two religions have been fighting each other from the time they first existed, and they disagree over many things, including what they mean by 'God'. Though both parties believe in 'God', they do not believe in the same God.

How, then, are we to consider the question 'Does God exist?'

*We cannot discuss whether or not God exists until we are clear in our minds about what we mean by 'God'.*

*     *     *

How shall we find a definition of God that fairly represents what those who say he exists really believe in?

The only fair way is to ask the believers themselves. They surely must know what it is they believe in, and so they can tell us. But which believers shall we ask? The Christian and the Hindu believe different things, and if we ask for a clear definition, either of them is likely to say that God is so great he cannot be defined.

Believers often say that God is mysterious and beyond human understanding. It is perfectly reasonable for someone to say that he cannot understand the nature of God; indeed, he would be arrogant to pretend he did. But, though he may not fully *understand* God, he still must know what this 'God' is that he says he believes in.

*If a man cannot say what God is, then the statement that he believes in God is practically meaningless.*

Other believers are very ready to define the kind of God they believe in. But these people contradict each other, depending upon which religion they belong to and which sect or group within that religion they happen to follow. And so, instead of having no clear definition, we are offered a thousand different definitions.

We cannot agonise indefinitely about the problem, but we have to resolve it. Let us therefore turn to a respected standard dictionary, which cannot avoid giving us a definition. According to the Oxford English Dictionary, a 'god' is a "superhuman person (regarded as masculine) worshipped as having power over nature and the fortunes of mankind". That definition may not satisfy all believers, but we have reached it without prejudice and it will at least be acceptable to the vast majority of those who believe in some kind of god.

As soon as we turn to the dictionary, we find ourselves spelling the word 'god' with a small letter; that is because the lexicographer who wrote that entry was not thinking of any one particular God, but of the general idea of a god, and so he has given us a definition which expresses the essentials of the idea, common to most religions. His statement tells us very little about any god, but precisely for that reason it is as near to a common denominator as we are likely to come; it expresses a basic minimum that will be agreed by the great majority.

*A god is a superhuman person (regarded as masculine) worshipped as having power over nature and the fortunes of mankind.*

\*     \*     \*

Some religions teach that there are many gods. These are called 'polytheistic', from the Greek for 'many gods'. The ancient Egyptians, the Greeks and Romans, the Vikings and many other past civilisations have worshipped and sacrificed to a great number of gods. So did our own ancestors in Britain until they were converted to Christianity. Still today, especially in India, there are hundreds of millions of Hindus who recognise and worship a number of gods.

Other religions, mainly in the East, do not recognise any gods at all in the sense that we have defined. According to Taoism and Confucianism there is a supreme reality, but that reality is not a god. The Buddhists venerate holy men, such as the great Buddha Gautama, but they do not think he was a god (the word *buddha* means 'enlightened', and a *buddha* is a man who has achieved enlightenment). It does happen in the East that many people do in fact worship buddhas, gods and spirits, and in that way their common practice may resemble that of the polytheists, but it is not the proper teaching of their religions.

There are also religions which teach that there is only one god. These are called 'monotheistic', from the Greek for 'one god'. The most important of them are Judaism, Christianity and Islam. The followers of these religions write the word 'God' with a capital letter, because they believe that there is only one God. Monotheists constitute only a minority of the religious believers in the world: the majority either believe in many gods, like the Hindus, or they belong to one of the religions which do not have a god at all.

The three great religions which have only one God belong together, because Christianity and Islam are both derived from the ancient religion of the Jews. Although the Jews had originally believed in many gods, they later came to worship only one god, called Yahweh (now better known as Jehovah), who was the protector of the Jewish people. Eventually, they came to believe that he was the only true God. That idea was taken over by the Christians and Muslims when they developed their own new religions out of the old Jewish religion. Thus, the one God who is now worshipped by the Christians and the Muslims was originally the God of the Jews.

Over a thousand million people, almost a third of the world's population, are reckoned to be Christians. Most of these (about 60%) are Roman Catholics. They would all agree that the God they believe in is the God proclaimed by their Church, that is, according to the *Catholic Encyclopaedia*, "the one Supreme and Infinite Personal Being, the Creator and Ruler of the universe, to whom man owes obedience and worship".

But it is natural that Christian ideas about God have changed over the centuries, and they also vary from one church and denomination to another. Most Christians agree that God is the creator and sustainer of the universe, the ultimate source of all things, the maker and father of all human beings. They believe he is a supreme person, who has absolute knowledge and power, and that he is good, and loves his creatures. But there are also some Christians who find it difficult to believe all these different things, and a few do not like the idea of God being a person.

And so, when we discuss whether or not 'God' exists, we must have in mind first and foremost the traditional Christian God, because that is the idea of God most widely believed in and taught in our part of the world. The traditional idea represents the opinion of the great majority of believers. But we must also take account of the more general idea of a god as "a superhuman person worshipped as having power over nature and the fortunes of mankind", and we shall have to consider some modern conceptions of God which believers have turned to on finding their traditional God unacceptable. It is our business to consider not only whether the traditional Christian God exists, but whether there is any kind of god at all.

# How can we ask such questions?

People have believed in gods for thousands of years. For well over one thousand years, right up to our own time, almost everybody in our European civilisation has believed in the Christian God. Among them were many of the wisest and most learned men who ever lived.

How can we question what all those people believed?

\*　　　　\*　　　　\*

At one time almost everybody believed the world was flat. Up to the time of Copernicus everybody believed the sun went round the earth, and many went on believing that long after the time of Copernicus because the Church punished anyone who disagreed. For thousands of years everyone believed there were living spirits in trees and rivers, and the sun was a divine person who went across the sky every day. They went on believing the sun was a god until ancient philosophers proved that his movements were regular and predictable and so he evidently had no mind of his own.

At first, those people who questioned whether the sun-god really existed were punished for asking such questions. When Anaxagoras said that the sun was not really a god but a mass of fiery stone, he was banished from Athens and sent into exile. The authorities and the laws supported those who stuck to the old beliefs, just as authorities and laws in almost every country today still support those who accept the traditional beliefs. But, as real knowledge increased, it became more and more clear to most thinking people that the old belief in the sun-god was simply ridiculous. And then the laws were changed, or at least not enforced.

Thus, as real knowledge increased, society gradually gave up its old beliefs, and those who questioned what had always been believed were no longer punished for blasphemy.

In the same way, most people have believed throughout the whole of human history, until a few hundred years ago, that this earth was the centre of the universe. But at the end of the Middle Ages, especially after the writings of Copernicus became known, it became clear to philosophers and scientists that the earth is only a planet going round the sun. Copernicus himself never dared to argue with the old belief except in his secret writings, and long after his death Galileo was silenced and imprisoned for saying that Copernicus had been right. But in time it became clear to thinking people that the old belief was wrong; those who questioned the traditional beliefs were then no longer suppressed and persecuted, but accepted and respected.

Thus, as knowledge advances, society is compelled to give up some of its old beliefs and to tolerate the opinions of those who no longer believe them.

*The fact that something has been believed for thousands of years is not a good reason for believing it now.*

*We are not any more clever than the people who believed those things; but we do now have a lot more reliable information about the world at our disposal, and that information can help us decide what is true. We now have the tools to observe the world far more closely, and the results of such observations have been collected and handed down over centuries. Our ancestors did not have that advantage. Consequently, we have no excuse for still believing many of the things that they believed.*

\*         \*         \*

10

Believers often exaggerate when they claim to represent the great majority of people. If you count all the people in 'Christian' countries, including the millions who seldom think about religion and raise no open objection to it, then the believers certainly do appear to be the great majority. But there is no proper reason why the millions who are indifferent to the question should be counted as believers.

In the past the proportion of real believers was larger; but then people had no choice. There was enormous pressure upon everyone to conform to the official religion and there were terrible punishments for anyone who did not. Throughout the history of Christianity, until a secular culture developed in the 17th and 18th centuries, disbelievers and heretics were imprisoned, subjected to hideous tortures, and usually killed; their writings were suppressed and burned. Yet in spite of these extreme pressures and penalties, there always were brave people who dared to reject the official beliefs, and at certain times in history when there was more freedom, such as in ancient Greece and Rome or in 18th-century Europe, a large number of the leading writers and thinkers did dare to speak out against religious belief. Some, like Voltaire, Spinoza or Thomas Paine, refused to believe in the personal God of Christianity or Judaism; others, like Democritus, Hobbes, Feuerbach, Marx and many others, refused to believe in any kind of gods at all.

Most people in most ages have believed in God. But does their number prove that they were right? Is truth a democratic thing, to be decided by counting the numbers on each side?

A thousand lemmings can't all be wrong, can they?

*We should never be impressed by the **number** of people who believe something. Any number of people can be wrong. Instead, we should pay attention to the **reasons** they have for their beliefs.*

In the past, religious beliefs which everybody had accepted for thousands of years have passed away, as the age-old worship of Osiris or the religions of Greece and Rome have passed away.

It is a slow process, because nations, like people, are slow and reluctant to change their minds. The social institutions of a nation are developed from its beliefs, and the authorities are usually afraid that the order of society will collapse if its traditional beliefs are undermined.

But beliefs and institutions gradually do change. After many centuries the Greeks outgrew their faith in the gods on Mount Olympus, gods who had been worshipped and sacrificed to by all the people for longer than anybody could possibly remember.

The pattern may equally well be observed in China. The earliest Chinese were very religious and worshipped many gods. But when they had developed a great civilisation, in the age of Lao-Tse and Confucius, the majority of educated people no longer believed in any gods at all. When it is said that most people everywhere have believed, we should remember that belief was always strongest among backward and primitive nations, and it has been weakest in the advanced civilisations of ancient China, Greece and Rome, and modern Europe.

There have always been people who questioned traditional beliefs. When the old beliefs could no longer be convincingly defended those people were listened to and the beliefs had to be rejected. Society had outgrown them. Today there are people who believe that our society has outgrown the traditional beliefs of Christianity, including the belief in the existence of God. Every one of us has to decide whether those people are right; and we must decide not by counting numbers but by considering the arguments and the evidence for their case.

*The **number** of believers proves nothing, but it does make sense to consider who they are. Are they people we respect?*

*Among those who believe in the Christian God there are many great and famous people, including politicians and writers, artists and broadcasters; but among those who have refused to believe there are such thinkers as Hume and Russell, scientists such as Darwin, Freud, Einstein, Madame Curie and Andrei*

*Sakharov, philanthropists like Florence Nightingale and Fritjof Nansen, writers like Voltaire and Goethe, Mark Twain and H. G. Wells, statesmen like Thomas Jefferson and Abraham Lincoln, broadcasters like Ludovic Kennedy and Magnus Magnusson, even churchmen and theologians such as D. F. Strauss and Michael Goulder, who gave up their place in the Church because they could not believe. These too are people whose judgment we must respect.*

*Clearly, there are people we respect on both sides of the debate. And so, in the end, there is nothing we can do but look at the evidence ourselves and draw our own conclusions.*

*       *       *

When we are not sure what to believe it is natural that we first turn to others who are likely to know better than we do. We would be foolish not to listen to other people. But precisely on important subjects people wiser than ourselves often have a variety of quite different opinions. We must listen to them and consider what they say; but in the end we will have to decide for ourselves which of them to believe, and what we can believe.

*When other people disagree you have to decide with your own mind, because your own mind is the only mind you have got.*

*Even if you decide to adopt someone else's beliefs, it still is your own decision whether or not to adopt them, and whether to adopt the beliefs of one person rather than another. There is no way you can escape deciding for yourself what to believe.*

*       *       *

The problem confronts us especially in childhood, when we begin our education by learning from our elders and following their example. We have to regard our elders as an authority and their word must carry weight.

But we cannot accept *everything* our elders and betters believe. When they say they believe in God, perhaps we should consider what they mean by 'believe'. Do they really take God seriously as a fact, or do they just vaguely feel that he is something they ought to 'believe in'?

When you were ill, did your parents immediately say their prayers, or did they first ring for the doctor? If they first rang for the doctor, doesn't that suggest that, deep inside, they had more faith in medical science than in God's response to prayers?

Perhaps they believe that religion is good, especially for the young, and they would like to think that their children have been well brought up. In that case they care more seriously about their children's education than about God.

*      *      *

Many people say God exists, but live their lives as though he did not. This prompts us to enquire how sincerely they believe. Is it possible to be indifferent to God's existence if you really believe he exists? If God is, for you, a reality, must you not constantly take that reality into account as you make the many decisions of your life?

From observing how a person behaves we can often infer what sort of things he believes. A man who jumps from an aeroplane clearly believes that parachutes work. When another man says they work but will not jump, we may be sure he has doubts. Does this not also apply to the person who says God exists, but does not in practical matters put his trust in God? If he really believed, then surely he would behave as if God were there and it would be foolish for him to ignore so important a fact. Are the true believers the many who say God exists or the few who show from their behaviour that they take that belief seriously?

The believer may object that his belief is perfectly real but not absolute: he has his doubts, but on balance he believes. He is like the reluctant parachutist who believes that his parachute works

14

but will not stake his life on it. That is a tenable and realistic position, and it explains why Christian believers do not flock to the bank to withdraw their savings and give to the poor.

But belief does not always entail great risks. The believer risks nothing by going to church, and if he thinks God exists it might be safer for him to go; yet many of those who say they believe are not regular churchgoers. Also, there are risks for the unbeliever if he should be proved wrong: if the Christian teaching is true and he has rejected it, then he can expect not only an embarrassing interview at the Pearly Gates but an eternity of torment thereafter. There are risks on either side for being wrong, and we may have to pay either for acting upon our beliefs or for failing to act.

We may fairly doubt the sincerity of the many who say they believe but live as if they did not, but we can never quite be sure, and so we have to allow them the benefit of the doubt. It may be that they do believe in God, but only feebly, and their belief is not sufficient to affect the way they live their lives.

$$* \qquad * \qquad *$$

When you consider what other people believe, you should always ask yourself *why* they believe it. Perhaps they were brought up to believe in God, or to think that all decent people believe. Perhaps they do not like to admit that they have doubts. But, even as a child, you cannot just take over other people's beliefs: you don't know which of the other people is right, or whether any of them at all is right. In the end you have to think things out for yourself and make up your own mind. That is what it means to grow up and become an independent person.

Many people, perhaps the majority, never learn to think for themselves. They simply copy the beliefs of the people around them without seriously considering whether or not they are correct; they do not choose their religion but receive it in the same way as they receive their nationality. And so, although many people believe, they believe different things according to the time and place where they happened to be born.

At one time everybody believed in many gods. Nowadays, most Europeans are Christian and believe in Jesus, while in the Middle East most people are Muslims and follow Muhammad. People generally have the same religion as their parents and neighbours. Thus, what a man believes is often decided not by the man himself, but by the accidents of geography and history.

Thinking for yourself is hard work. Most people prefer to copy the opinions and beliefs of the people around them. That is the easy path. Each of us has to decide whether or not to take this easy path, or whether to think things out for ourselves.

If we wish to regard ourselves as rational, thinking people, then, surely, we cannot merely adopt other people's opinions. A rationalist will want to find the truth, rather than accept what the people around him happen to believe, and so in his search for the truth he will have to make up his own mind.

*     *     *

To make up your own mind on the question of the existence of God means that you must consider the evidence for his existence and then judge for yourself whether that evidence convinces you. What is the evidence? What are the reasons which believers give when they are asked why they believe? These are the questions we must turn to next.

*A man must "proportion his belief to the evidence", as the great Scottish philosopher David Hume said.*

# Can we prove that God exists?

Until recently most Christians believed they could prove by logical reasoning that God exists. Many still do believe that, including orthodox Roman Catholics, for it is a dogma of the Catholic Church that God can be known through his creation and through human reason.

Some Christians nowadays disagree with that teaching. They have other ways of justifying their belief. But as long as the Catholic Church continues to teach that valid proofs exist, and many people continue to believe in them, it will be necessary for us to examine those proofs.

Although modern Christians may not always recognise the traditional arguments as **proofs** of God's existence, many of them still use those arguments as **evidence** which supports their faith. That is especially true of the 'Argument from Design', which states that by looking at the world around us and observing the beauty and order and the evidence of purpose in nature we can reasonably infer that it must have been made by a purposeful God. Believers will often invite us to look at the world of nature and see in it the work of God.

> The heavens declare the glory of God,
> And the firmament sheweth his handiwork. (*Psalm 19*)

It is understandable that those who believe in God see evidence of his activity in the world around them, and in this way they are still using the old 'Argument from Design', though as a corroboration and confirmation of their faith rather than as a compelling proof by itself.

While this 'Argument from Design' appeals to our experience of the world and calls upon us to recognise God's work in things we see, there are other kinds of 'proof' which depend not upon experience, but upon logic. These are less popular today, though they are often still used in one form or other. The most famous of these are the 'First Cause' and the 'ontological' arguments. We will look at them later, but first we must examine the 'Argument from Design', since it is the most widely accepted and influential of these arguments today.

## The Argument from Design

Evidence for order in the cosmos, in particular the regular motions of the heavenly bodies, was observed by the ancient Greeks and led some of their philosophers to conclude that the universe was the work of an intelligent Designer. Centuries later that argument was taken over by Christian thinkers, who derived many of their ideas from the Greeks.

The idea of God as a Designer who sustains the cosmos and directs its activity is beautifully expressed in an old hymn of St Ambrose (AD 340-397), which was translated thus long ago:

O God, the world's great Architect,
Who dost heavn's rowling Orbs direct,
Cloathing the day with beauteous light
And with sweet slumbers silent night.....

Ambrose, who wrote these lines, was the teacher of St Augustine, most important of all the Church Fathers, who knew the philosophy of the Greeks and did more than any man to establish the doctrines of the Christian Church.

Among the Greeks it was Plato's pupil Aristotle who taught, in the fourth century BC, that the regular motions of the visible cosmos imply the existence of an intelligent god. The main teachings of Aristotle became part of Christian philosophy in the Middle Ages, when St Thomas Aquinas worked out the system of Christian belief which is still today recognised as true and authoritative by the Roman Catholic Church and is very highly regarded by most others.

Aquinas adopted Aristotle's proof of the existence of God and it has been taught by Christians ever since. But Aristotle himself, when he argued that the ordered universe implies an intelligent god, could not possibly have had the Jewish or Christian God in mind (he knew nothing about the Jews and he lived three centuries before Christianity began). The god of Aristotle is not a person at all, but an intelligent power that exists at the heart of nature, a power that never changes and cannot ever intervene in human affairs, as the God of the Christians did when he created the world or when he sent Jesus to 'save' us. For Aristotle the world never was created, because he thought the world was eternal, and he could not have known about the God who directed the history of the Jews.

Aristotle's god is an abstraction, which by sheer existence causes material things to move. God did not create the order of nature and does not sustain it by any kind of action, but permanently inspires it by his being; he is an "unmoved mover", who "moves as one who is loved". Such a being is very different from the God of the Christians, and those people in Christian societies who have believed in Aristotle's kind of god have regularly been condemned as secret atheists.

The Church adopted Aristotle's proof in order to support its own Christian God, but in fact the argument of Aristotle, if it is valid at all, cannot prove anything more than an intelligent principle lying at the heart of nature. The orderly motion of stars and planets cannot prove that there is a God of love, who cares for his people Israel and sent his son Jesus for the benefit of mankind, a personal God who is aware of our existence and to whom it might make sense to pray.

A number of great thinkers who have refused to believe in the personal God of the Jews and Christians have nevertheless accepted the kind of God who is a principle working within nature, or who set the cosmos in motion but can never interfere in the course of history. These people are called Pantheists and Deists, and they include such men as Spinoza and Goethe, Paine and Voltaire. The great thinkers of the 18th century, who rebelled against an arbitrary God meddling in human affairs and sometimes suspending his own laws of nature, were attracted by the idea of a divine source of universal order which gave rise to nature and her laws.

*We must, therefore, consider whether the orderly motions and patterns which we observe in nature compel us to accept at least some kind of god, a god who is the cause of that motion and order.*

The argument that the order in the universe implies an intelligent God presupposes that chaos is more natural than order, so that order could only come about as a result of some intelligence. Is that true?

When we look at the sea, we may observe that the pebbles are not scattered at random in the water, but all lie at the bottom or on the shore. And when we look at the shore we may notice that the small stones lie near the water's edge while larger ones are higher up the beach.

Is that because a purposeful Mind has designed such an arrangement, or is it an inevitable consequence of the weight of the pebbles, the nature of water and the action of the tides, which grinds up large pebbles and makes smaller ones?

The stuff of which the universe is made must necessarily have some kind of characteristic features simply because it exists. We can observe the features of different kinds of matter and the way they interact with each other and respond to forces which act upon them. When we describe the way these things happen we call our definitions 'laws' of nature. According to

20

these 'laws', which describe things the way they happen to be, we may observe that heavy things fall while hot liquids evaporate and rise, and such processes necessarily produce a certain regularity and order. If the 'laws' of nature were different, they might produce a different kind of order. But the very fact that matter and energy exist at all, and therefore must have properties which make them interact in some particular way, a way we define as nature's 'laws' - that very fact of existence will tend to produce order, regardless of any governing intelligence and purpose.

It is sometimes argued that the laws of nature can only have been established by God. But that argument is only possible if we confuse two quite different meanings of the word 'law'.

A law of nature is not a rule which somebody made up to govern people: it is a description of the way things behave. When a pebble sinks to the bottom of the sea, that is not because someone (presumably God) ordained that there should be a law of gravity which pebbles must obey, but because stone is denser than water and so the water cannot resist the pebble's fall.

The tendency of heavy things to fall is simply a fact about the way things are: it has nothing at all to do with the kind of 'law' which one person makes and another must obey. It is a mere accident of language that we happen to use the same word in both cases. A 'law', meaning a social rule, does indeed presuppose a person who must have made it up, but a 'law', meaning a statement about the way things are, is something quite different and there is no reason at all to imagine it must have been laid down by some intelligent being who wanted to have order in his world.

*The argument that order must have been designed presupposes that the natural state of things is disorder. But that is not in fact what we observe in nature, and it is not what we ought to expect. Any real world must be ordered, at least to some extent, by the operation of whatever natural laws apply in that world;*

*those laws are nothing more than a statement of the way things behave, which is a result of what that world is made of.*

\*        \*        \*

If we look closely at a spider's web we can see that it forms a beautiful and intricate pattern. But that pattern is not the result of a planning intelligence in the mind of the spider. It is simply that, as the spider spins her web, it falls into a regular pattern. Though we may regard that pattern with pleasure, as a thing of beauty, the spider neither designs nor notices it. The tendency for things to fall into patterns is a fact which, far from surprising us and requiring a supernatural explanation, should be expected to follow from whatever nature things might have.

It is possible, then, to account for the cosmic patterns in the universe without the hypothesis of a Designer. Indeed, if we did choose to explain them by using that hypothesis, we should then have to explain how the idea of order and the will to impose it upon things ever came to be in the mind of the Designer. That might be difficult.

But the 'Argument from Design' does not rely on the observation of cosmic order alone. It also points to the highly intricate arrangements of living things, in which the parts seem to be ordered so as to serve some greater purpose, so that the organism as a whole is capable of survival. In this form the Argument is more suited to Christianity, because it argues not for the Aristotelian abstraction called 'God' but for a benevolent and purposeful Designer such as the Christian God.

\*        \*        \*

A famous Christian version of the 'Argument from Design' is associated with the Anglican clergyman William Paley, who taught it at the end of the 18th century.

Paley said that if a man picked up a stone as he was crossing a heath he might imagine it had always been there, but if he picked up a watch he would have to conclude that somebody must have designed it, because the structure of a watch provides evidence of purposeful design. But the parts of a flower or an animal, and the parts of the human body, such as the eye, also serve a purpose beyond themselves and they are much more cleverly designed than any watch. So somebody must have designed them. That somebody we call God.

*Is Paley right to compare the world of nature with a watch and draw his conclusion that both must have been designed?*

Paley himself points out that the watch is strikingly different from the heath. But if everything that exists has been designed by God, then the watch should be like the heath, not different from it. The heath, the watch, the flowers or the human eye - all of them would have been designed. But in fact the watch strikes us as different, and that is why we assume that it was designed and the heath was not.

We have seen watches before, and we know they are always made by designers. But we do not know that about the heath. We also know that the watch was designed for a purpose. But we do not know that the heath was designed for any purpose.

Paley says we can see the watch is designed because it is clearly different from the heath which was not designed. But God is not supposed to be like a man who lives on a heath and designs things: he is supposed to have made the heath as well. The designer of a watch only re-arranges materials which already existed. But God is supposed to have 'created' the materials out of nothing, and that is very different from designing.

It is easy to make up a word 'create' and let it mean 'to make something out of nothing'. But as far as we know it is not possible to make something out of nothing. A designer only makes something out of something else.

*Never be tricked into believing a thing is real just because language has a word for it.*

*We have words for 'creation', and 'God', just as we have words for mermaids, fairies and sugar-candy mountains. Words are easily invented for anything that we can imagine. But what we imagine is not necessarily real.*

*When words have been invented, we are tempted to take for granted that the things or processes they refer to really exist. That is why people are disposed to talk seriously about such things as telepathy or communication with the spirit world: the existence of the right words makes it easy for us to consider and talk about such things, and we are easily tricked into taking their real existence for granted.*

*In the same way we are disposed to take seriously the idea that we were created by God because, in the languages which we have inherited from our religious-minded ancestors, we have words which enable us to think about these things as if they were real.*

*         *         **

There is a kind of false argument which logicians call the 'petitio principii', or begging the question: it consists in taking for granted the very thing which the argument is supposed to prove. It is easy to be fooled by this kind of argument because it takes you off your guard: before you begin to think about the question you have been tricked into accepting something that points to one particular answer. When Christians use the term 'Argument from Design' they are committing the offence of *petitio principii* because the very name they give to their 'proof' takes for granted that there is design in the universe. We are then invited to explain how that design came about. Surely there must have been a Designer?

But in fact we do not know whether there is design in nature: what we observe is not design, but order, pattern and symmetry. Whether that order came about as a result of design, or by some other process, is the very question we have to decide. It is not an assumption we can take for granted before we start thinking about it.

The Christian believes that the patterns were designed by God, and so he invites us to explain the existence of the 'design': if he can get us talking about 'design' rather than 'order' we shall come to the conclusion that there must be a Designer. For that reason Professor Flew says this argument should be called the 'Argument *to* Design', not the 'Argument *from* Design'.

\*           \*           \*

Paley's argument was that the evidence for design which we see in a watch presupposes a designer, and that there is similar evidence for design in the universe as a whole. But, as we have seen, his 'parallel' between a watch and the universe is not really parallel. That is usually the trouble with drawing conclusions from 'parallels': when you look at them closely you discover that they are not really parallel at all.

The watch is a thing *within* the universe which somebody made by re-arranging things that already existed. The universe itself is different: we cannot explain its existence by saying that somebody re-arranged its parts.

It is not the complexity of the watch, or even the purposefulness of its parts, that makes us sure it has been made by a designer. A flower is just as complex as a watch, and its various parts work excellently together, yet if we found a flower on the heath we would not at once be sure it had been made by a designer. That is because flowers, and many other complex things, are found naturally on the heath, while a watch is known to be an artificial thing that does not belong there. We know very well that a watch is designed for a purpose, but we do not know that about the heath, or the flowers upon it, or about the whole of nature or the universe.

The vital difference between a watch and a living organism is that a watch does not grow as living things grow.

A watch does not begin its career as a little seed and then grow bigger; it does not eventually make seeds of its own which grow into little watches. Each watch is complete, full-sized and working when it is made. That is why we assume that it was designed by an intelligent maker. Living things are different.

Every animal, every plant, every living part of every living thing is always changing. It grows and it decays. Each animal or plant produces offspring, and the offspring are not quite the same as the parents. Though each individual plant or animal dies, the species goes on; and precisely because the offspring are different from the parents, the species develops and changes.

By choosing the most suitable parents, breeders have been able to develop fast racehorses, and all kinds of dogs, fat sheep and juicy fruits that would otherwise never have existed. That is done by people, who carefully and  deliberately select the features they want to develop and breed together animals or plants which happen to have those features.

Could that sort of thing have happened by accident? Could simple cells of living matter have developed into animals with great physical and mental powers, so that now they look as if some marvellous intelligence must have designed them?

Charles Darwin taught us the answer over a century ago, when he published his famous book *On the Origin of Species by Natural Selection*.

\*        \*        \*

Every plant and animal species produces far more offspring than could possibly survive in a world of limited resources. Most plants and animals produce as many offspring as they can. Consequently, all living things are constantly engaged in a struggle for existence.

Within each species the individuals also must compete for partners with which to mate and produce their offspring. If one animal happens to have some advantage, such as better eyesight, sharper ears or more intelligence than the others, then that animal is likely to live longer and produce more offspring. The offspring inherit characteristics from their parents. So, over a long period of time, those characteristics which happen to prove useful and advantageous in the struggle for existence will become more common - they will have been inherited by a larger number - and those which prove to be handicaps will tend to die out. In this way every species will keep on being improved, entirely by accident.

The constant changing of all species is called 'evolution'. Darwin explained the progress of evolution with his argument that those individuals that are best fitted to survive, perhaps the strongest, or fastest, or cleverest of them, will naturally tend to live longer and have more offspring which can pass on their parents' strength, or speed, or cleverness to another generation. He called the process 'evolution by natural selection'. By that term he made it clear that the process is a natural one, in contrast to the artificial selection practised by breeders who wish to change some of the characteristics of a species deliberately.

Artificial selection produces changes in quite a short time. Natural selection takes much longer.

All life forms on this earth are constantly changing through the process of evolution which is guided by natural selection. That process takes much longer than a breeder would take using artificial selection, because in nature those lucky accidents which happen to improve the chances of survival and successful mating are rare. But it doesn't matter how long it takes, because there is no shortage of time. We know from the fossils of prehistoric organisms that there has been life on this earth for over three thousand million years, and for most of that time only the most primitive life-forms existed.

It has been wisely said that the secret of nature's success is her infinite patience. She takes her time.

Such marvellous and complex things as a living animal, or the human eye, or even a single protein cell, could not have come into existence all at once, as a result of a single accident; the fossil record shows us that these things arose out of far more primitive forms only very gradually, over thousands of millions of years, through countless billions of accidents, most of which produced no remarkable result at all, or else produced evolutionary failures which quickly disappeared from the world of nature.

*         *         *

In the course of evolution, many millions of species, from dinosaurs to dodos, have died out completely. These were the ones that did not happen to adapt, or could not compete with other species which did adapt. They are the victims of the process of evolution by natural selection.

The fact that there have been so many victims is exactly what you would expect from a process that happens by accident. But it is not what you would expect if God had designed those creatures with a purpose. Each of those creatures had been the climax of many millions of years of evolution; it might have appeared that the long years of slow progress that had led up to them had been guided by a benevolent God: but then they just died and became extinct.

If you wish to believe that all living things were deliberately created by God, then you have a number of awkward questions to answer. For example:

> *Why did God design so many species which just died out?*
> *Why so much waste?*
>
> *Why did God start by designing simple cells and primitive life forms, which would ultimately lead up to the higher*

28

*animals, rather than design the higher animals in the first place?*

*Why did he design man with a useless appendix, or the whale with teeth which he never uses?*

*Why design so many animals just to have most of them kill each other for food, or else die miserably from diseases caused by organisms which he also created?*

*Was it God's deliberate purpose that there should be so much pain?*

*If the human eye is a perfect example of God's creation, why am I wearing spectacles?*

If you wish to praise God for the design, should you not also blame him for the faults in the design?

In the course of evolution there have been far more failures than successes. Only a few of the hardiest species have survived. Any human designer with that kind of failure rate would not get a reputation for absolute wisdom and power, and he certainly would not get worshipped. He would get the sack.

*       *       *

*It is generally considered bad form to criticise God's work in this way. But if God made this world and all its creatures, having absolute power and free will to make it differently if he so desired, then it is fair and reasonable to ask why he made nature as it is, so full of misery, pain and waste, when he could have made the world differently.*

*When the American atheist campaigner R. G. Ingersoll made this point at a public meeting, he was asked to declare how he would improve upon God's creation if he were creating the world. He replied: "I would make good health infectious, instead of diseases."*

*Both the question and the answer are fair. If we are going to think seriously about God there is no reason why we should feel it is bad taste to question his supposed behaviour.*

*A hundred years ago, when good form was considered more important than it usually is today, W. K. Clifford wrote: "Truth is a thing to be shouted from the housetops, not to be whispered over the walnuts and wine after the ladies have left . . . for only by plain and honest speech on this matter can liberty of thought be won."*

\*     \*     \*

Understandably, when we consider for a moment the great complexity of the universe and the wonders of living things, it is hard to believe that all this 'just happened'. Surely, we may think, so many wonderful things must have been made deliberately, by some great Intelligence. But, if we take that view, we must explain whether that great Intelligence 'just happened' to be, or whether it was made deliberately by another, still greater Intelligence. And so on.

Intelligence is not a simple thing, like a stone or an elementary particle: we find it only in some complex, highly developed organism, such as the human brain, on which it depends for its existence. We have no evidence that intelligence ever could exist by itself, springing up out of nowhere. It is therefore hard to imagine how there could have been any kind of intelligence at all before the first animals were born, let alone a divine Intelligence capable of creating the whole universe and all life.

People who say that God 'just happened' to exist, without being 'created', cannot then reasonably argue that the world is too complicated to exist without having been created. If we can believe that a God capable of creating the whole complex universe could have 'just happened' to be, then we could more simply believe that the particles of which the universe is made just happened to be, and that those particles evolved into more

30

complex forms in the course of billions of years. Astounding as the world of nature may seem today, we can more easily explain how it grew out of simple beginnings than explain how a great Intelligence arose out of nothing and made it.

When we look with wonder upon the things of nature and find it hard to credit that they could possibly have come about through a series of blind accidents, then we should also consider the immensity of the time-scale which nature required to produce those results, a time-scale which is equally stupendous. The two are commensurate.

We should also observe that, as we look back along that time-scale, so the natural organisms whose origin we wish to explain become more simple and elementary, and so our problem melts away as we follow the time dimension back. We can see how complex forms arose out of simple ones, as we should expect if all of them evolved by natural selection, and as we should not expect if they had all been created by an intelligent God.

We might even presume to ask, if God's purpose was to produce higher intelligence capable of salvation and able to praise him, why it is that the earth had no intelligent life for most of its history, and every other planet we know appears to be completely barren, rather than filled with intelligent life. If the conditions necessary for life arose by accident then we can understand that the accident only happened here, but if life was God's purpose, we might expect to see evidence of his purpose on the other planets too. (It may be, of course, that planets not yet discovered may also support life; but if they do, that will be evidence of chance, which may occur more than once, rather than evidence of an intelligent planner who might have populated all the planets.)

According to the Bible and the whole Christian tradition, the purpose for which God made us is that we should worship and glorify him. The animals were made to be of service to man, and man was made to praise God. In this Christianity agrees with other religions: the world is covered with mosques and temples, churches and chapels, where believers meet to praise and glorify their particular God, and none of them doubts that this is what God really wants. And yet it seems curious that the God who made the whole cosmos should wish to be worshipped by the likes of us and created the physical universe and the entire animal kingdom so as to make it possible. In some past age that may have seemed a credible hypothesis to explain the existence of life and the universe; but is it a credible hypothesis now?

*         *         *

Some plants and animals are beautiful. Is that because God designed them beautifully? Or is 'beauty' an emotion inside ourselves, something which we feel when we experience certain things?

There is a difficulty about looking at all the beautiful things in the world and saying they must have been made by God. The world also contains many ugly and horrible things. If God made all things bright and beautiful, then he also made all things dark and horrible.

If the beauty of the tiger comes from God, doesn't his savage cruelty also come from God? If God made him beautiful because he loves beauty, did he also make him cruel because he loves cruelty? The poet William Blake thinks of God contemplating the tiger he has created and asks:

Did he smile his work to see?
Did he that made the lamb make thee?

If you are going to draw conclusions about God by looking at the world of nature, then you will soon have reason to think that God must love pain and cruelty very much indeed.

In fact, if you draw conclusions about God from looking at nature, then you might think there was not just one Designer, who made all creatures great and small, but a whole lot of Designers, all warring with each other and trying to design animals that

32

would destroy the ones which another Designer had made. When one God said 'Let there be flies!', a rival God said 'Let there be spiders!', and then another said 'Let there be birds!'. But that is *not* what Christian thinkers were trying to prove by their Argument from Design.

If you believe that God made all the things in nature, and that God deliberately arranged nature so that his creatures live by eating each other alive, then the God you will have to believe in will not be a God of love, but a horrible sadistic monster. The teeth and jaws of the wolf are remarkably well suited for the tearing of sheep; but what are we to think of a Designer who had that in mind?

*The design may seem excellent from the point of view of the wolf. But is it excellent from the point of view of the sheep?*

With Darwin's theory of evolution by natural selection we can explain how each species has acquired certain features which serve its own advantage and help it to survive. Thus we can understand the teeth and jaws of the wolf. Such things cannot be explained with the hypothesis of a benevolent God who cares for all his creatures.

*       *       *

Another 'proof' that nature was designed by God is the fact that this world is constructed just right for human beings to live in it. We have water and air, and just enough gravity, just enough warmth - a bit closer to the sun and we would burn, a bit further away and we would freeze. The laws of nature also seem designed in a way that suits our convenience. The chances that those conditions would have arisen by accident are very tiny.

Quite so! If the world were different, we would not exist in it. Some other life-form might have evolved instead, beings perhaps that needed ammonia instead of air, and liked boiling hot temperatures and not much gravity. Those beings would look at the world and say: "Gosh! Exactly the conditions we need for our kind of existence! It must have been designed by a God."

In *some* places, admittedly, no life of any kind would be possible. No life-forms are evolving on the surface of the sun. But in all those places where life *can* exist, the forms of life that have evolved are determined by the conditions that happened to be there. That is why squirrels do not live in the sea and whales are seldom found in the branches of trees. The sea was not made for whales to live in, but whales developed in the sea. Our world was not 'created' the way it is to suit the convenience of people like us. Instead, our ancestors survived because they were the animals that fitted in best with the kind of world which they found themselves in.

The world existed for many millions of years before it had any forms of life in it at all. And when at last the most primitive life forms did begin to emerge, then those that survived were, naturally, the forms which were best able to survive in the world as it happened to be. When conditions changed, some forms died out and were replaced by others which fitted in better with the new conditions. That is why dinosaurs disappeared and mammals prospered. No God made the world on purpose for us, but the living things which have flourished in the world were those best suited to the kind of world it actually was.

Purpose and design are easy to find if you look for them. The great French writer Voltaire once wrote that God designed the human nose exactly right for supporting spectacles.

\*        \*        \*

By the way ................... Who designed God?

# The 'Ontological Proof'

The 'Argument from Design' appeals to our experience. It invites us to look at the regular patterns and complex living organisms that exist in the world and infer from what we observe that they must have been made by an intelligent God. There is another kind of argument that appeals to our powers of reasoning and claims to prove by logical argument that God must exist. The most famous of these is known as the 'ontological proof'.

Ontology is the study of the philosophy of being. And so to prove God exists 'ontologically' is remarkably like saying that he is because he is. Therefore, as we examine this proof, we must be on the look-out for circular arguments.

The ontological proof was formulated in the 11th century by St Anselm, a scholastic philosopher who taught it to his students at Paris. Though St Thomas Aquinas rejected it, it was later revived and revised, especially by Descartes, and has been taught in many thousands of schools ever since.

It states that everyone, even the unbeliever, has in his mind the idea of God and knows that this God is the most perfect being we can think of. But if that most perfect being were lacking existence it would be less than perfect. Therefore God exists.

*In other words: "If you can think of a perfect Being you must believe in his existence, because if he did not exist he would not be perfect."*

*　　　*　　　*

Now that you have considered the ontological proof for a while, are you convinced that God exists? Did the ontological proof persuade you, as it persuaded St Anselm and his students? Of course it did not. The fact that I can think of a perfect being (even

35

if it is true that I can) does not prove that such a being really exists. That is obvious to anyone today. So why was it not obvious to St Anselm and his students?

The reason is: the students of St Anselm were convinced because they desperately wanted and needed to be convinced, and they found the ontological proof a helpful argument to justify their belief. They were, after all, students of theology and future servants of the Church. Even today the argument may seem attractive to people who desperately want to believe. But to most of us it is clear that we can think of dragons and fairies, wombles and mumintrolls, we can imagine flying pigs and sugar-candy mountain, even the most perfect of all imaginable sugar-candy mountains. We can imagine a cosmic person called God and define him as the greatest being that exists. But that doesn't make him exist in reality.

The sort of existence which the greatest being imaginable must have is an imaginary existence. If I imagine God as perfect, and assume that perfection includes existence, then I must imagine him as existing. But that does not prove whether he really exists or not.

Certainly, if I define 'God' in such a way as to include existence, then it would be irrational of me to say 'God does not exist'. That would imply 'an existing being does not exist'. But when I correct that error and say 'an existing being exists', my words are still nothing more than a statement, and may be either true or false.

\*     \*     \*

Sometimes the 'ontological proof' is paraphrased: "God is perfect, therefore God is." But that is just playing with words. The first "is" means 'has an attribute', while the second "is" means 'exists'. It just so happens that the English language uses the word 'is' to express those two different meanings. But many languages do not have a word with those two senses; for example, there is no word in French that means both 'is, has an attribute' and 'is, exists'. You cannot say in French "God is perfect, therefore God is" without using two different words for 'is', because 'is' means two different things. That sort of argument is not a proof, but a trick with words.

Another version of the ontological proof states that because God is perfect he must have all conceivable attributes (or 'predicates', as philosophers say). Therefore, he must have the attribute of existence.

Is it possible that any being could have all conceivable attributes? Does God have the attribute of badness, as well as that of goodness? Is he fat, square, triangular and round, as well as red, green, transparent, waterproof and invisible? If God has all conceivable attributes, then surely he must be full of quite impossible contradictions.

Even two attributes may be enough to produce contradiction. It is generally agreed that God is both just and merciful. But while his justice requires him to punish the sinner, his mercy requires him to forgive. We may fudge the problem, as St Bernard of Clairvaux did, by claiming that God appeased his justice by sacrificing his own innocent Son, at whose Cross mercy and justice were reconciled. That solution is elegant and has an emotional appeal, but it is hardly rational: for it would be a strange kind of justice that wilfully punishes the innocent in place of the guilty. In fact, the problem cannot be solved, because the two attributes make contradictory demands. The contradictions within God will become far greater if we give him all conceivable attributes.

\*    \*    \*

Anyway, existence is not really an attribute at all. An attribute tells us what something is like ('big', 'green', 'powerful') or what it has (e.g. a cat has a tail), but 'existence' is a word meaning that something exists. If we say God has existence, we do not mean that he has some attribute, but that he (with all his attributes) exists.

We may adapt an example from the philosopher G.E. Moore: It makes sense to say 'some cats have tails and others do not', but it makes no sense at all to say 'some cats have existence and others do not'. How can there be a cat that lacks existence? That would be simply no cat.

Bertrand Russell made the point very clearly in his discussion of the 'ontological proof'. He said that when we say 'a cow exists' and 'a unicorn does not exist', we do not mean that there are two animals, one of which is deficient in existence. We mean that the concept of 'a cow', together with all its attributes, corresponds to something that exists, while that of 'a unicorn' does not. In other words, there is an instance of a cow, but there is not an instance of a unicorn.

Thus, we may imagine God as perfect as we like and give him all possible attributes, but existence is not one of them. The question of his existence simply means: 'Is there a God?'

And that is the point. If we wish, we may say 'God has everything', but still we have to ask 'Is there a God?'

\*　　　　　\*　　　　　\*

Logic draws conclusions from premisses, that is, propositions which it assumes are true. Thus, if all dogs have noses, and Fido is a dog, logic can prove that Fido has a nose. But a logical argument cannot prove its own premisses. They are its starting point, and if they are wrong, then the conclusion is likely to be wrong.

It is logical for me to argue that, if all dogs have three noses, and Fido is a dog, then Fido has three noses. There is nothing wrong with the logic. But there is something wrong with one of the premisses.

The 'ontological' argument assumes as its premisses that God is perfect and that perfection includes existence. Quite logically, it argues: If all perfect things exist, and God is perfect, then God exists.

But how do we know that the premisses are true?

*     *     *

Some of the most important philosophers who tried to prove by reasoning that God exists, such as St Thomas Aquinas and Immanuel Kant, rejected the ontological proof because they did not consider it a proper proof at all. They abandoned it and looked for other proofs.

The word 'ontological' sounds impressive and therefore profound. But we must never be persuaded by impressive words when we do not accept the argument or see the reality behind them. It is easy to use the word pretentiously (as a philosopher once pointed out, when he defined a liar as 'a person who wilfully misplaces his ontological predicates').

It is ridiculous to say that God exists just because I can imagine him. But somehow it does not sound quite so ridiculous when you call it the 'ontological proof'.

What is the lesson to be learnt?

*Never be taken in by impressive words!*

## The First Cause

The great problem with the 'ontological proof' was that it attempted to prove God's existence by pure reasoning. But, as we have seen, reasoning is always dependent upon its premisses, and in this case we have no way of knowing that the premisses are true.

That danger is avoided in another kind of argument, known as the 'First Cause'; for, although it also depends upon reasoning, its premiss is the principle of causation, and that is a principle which we derive from our observation of things in this world.

The argument runs like this: Everything that happens in the world has a cause. The cause also had a cause. And so on. But something must have happened in the first place to start the chain of causation moving. That must have been the First Cause. And the First Cause we call God.

It is God who started everything moving. God set all the stars and planets moving in their orbits through the sky. God created the ancestors of all living species (or, if you believe in evolution, then it was God who started the process going). God was the beginning of all history.

It sounds good. But is it really necessary to believe there was a First Cause? And if so, how do we know that cause was God?

*       *       *

If you argue that every cause has a cause, then it is not logical to believe in a First Cause which did not have any cause. You have to face the question: What caused the First Cause? If you believe the First Cause was God, then the question becomes: Who made God? That is a question that religions are not good at answering.

*The argument that every cause had a cause will carry the believer back through the chain of causation until he reaches the First Cause, which he calls 'God'. Then, having arrived safely at his destination, he is satisfied and forgets that every cause has a cause. The argument is, as Schopenhauer said, like a cab which may be dismissed when it has carried us where we want to go.*

Christian philosophers since St Augustine have tried to avoid this problem by saying that God created the chain of causation when he created the universe. God did not have a cause, and did not need to have one, since causes are something he created. But if God did not need to have a cause, then perhaps the universe did not need one either. If God just pre-existed before he created the universe, then perhaps the stuff of the universe could have just pre-existed, before it collected into suns and planets.

*If God had pre-existed for an infinite amount of time before he created the universe, what was it that caused him to change his mind and create it? Strictly, if we are looking for a First Cause, it should not be a pre-existing God, but whatever it was that caused God to change his previously eternal pattern of behaviour and create the universe.*

*If the pre-existing God was perfect without being a creator, what made him decide to become a creator? Was he then even more perfect?*

*Charles Bradlaugh pointed out that it is illogical to try to "prove an immutable Deity by demonstrating a mutation on the part of Deity".*

\*            \*            \*

The argument is sometimes expressed in terms of motion rather than cause. We may then be asked to think of a long goods train. Every wagon on the train is moved by the one immediately in front of it, which pulls it along, because none of the wagons can move by itself. But the whole train of wagons would not move at all if there were not, at the very beginning of the chain, something which pulls without being pulled. Thus, the real cause of all the motion is the 'Unmoved Mover' at its beginning.

It makes little difference whether the argument is expressed in terms of causality (cause and effect) or of motion (pulling and being pulled). In either case it is assumed that nothing happens without a cause (or: nothing moves by itself) and that the chain is not infinite. For if the train were infinitely long, there would be no wagon that was not being pulled by a wagon in front (or: no cause without a prior cause).

41

It might be objected that a train of infinite length would not be in motion if nothing pulled it (or: a causal chain of infinite length must first have been activated). That objection would have been compelling in the Middle Ages, when the 'First Cause' argument was undisputed, because it was also undisputed that the natural state of all things is to be at rest and nothing can move unless it is set in motion. But one of the great achievements of Galileo was to prove that the natural state of things is not a state of rest, but a state of constant motion. Such motion, therefore, does not require a cause.

Another premiss of the argument is that everything that happens in the world is the necessary effect of a cause. That assumption was very effectively criticised by Hume in the 18th century and scientists and philosophers today are careful to avoid taking it for granted. The familiar rules of cause and effect do not always apply, for example, in the world of subatomic particles and quantum physics.

When we speak of 'cause' and 'effect' we assume that two events, one of which regularly follows the other in time, are *necessarily* linked so that the one *must* follow the other. But we have no way of observing or proving that the sequence of events which we have regularly observed is a necessary one and always must occur in circumstances which cannot be observed. The idea of causation is a very useful theory, which helps us to deal with the practical affairs of this world: but it is not a certain and provable fact from which to draw conclusions about tiny events within the atom or huge events such as the beginning of the world.

\*       \*       \*

Even if we did decide to trace all history back to a First Cause, we still should not have any reason for thinking that this First Cause was some kind of person whom we may call God, rather than, say, a great explosion that sent the stars and planets into

42

their orbits. We also should have no reason for thinking that the Cause which set the universe in motion is an eternal cause, and therefore still in existence today, rather than a singular event that happened long ago. We can see through our modern telescopes that all the galaxies are moving away from each other. That looks more like the result of a great explosion some time in the past than the result of a good, loving, all-seeing, all-powerful Person who somehow had just been there all along and then decided to start everything going, a Person who still exists and loves us.

We do not really know how everything began, though scientists are trying hard to find out and they have their theories about it. There is not enough evidence to prove that any one of these theories is true. But the fact that we do not know is not a reason for assuming, without any evidence at all, that everything must have resulted from one cause, and that cause must have been God.

### The Moral Argument

Some people say there must be a God because there is morality. We do not always behave as we should, but we do have a natural sense of what is right and wrong, so that we generally know how we *ought* to behave, even if nobody tells us. Sometimes our own moral sense conflicts which what we are told and makes us want to rebel against authority. This moral sense must have come from somewhere, and its source must be a moral power outside of ourselves. That moral power we call God.

The philosopher Immanuel Kant, after he had demonstrated that the Argument from Design, the ontological proof and the 'First Cause' argument are not valid, went on to conclude that the only true reason we have for believing in the existence of God is our own morality, which would not be justified if there were no God. Kant, however, is very cautious about this. He says that our moral nature makes it necessary for us to believe in God, but he avoids saying plainly that God actually exists, and he rejects the idea that our moral sense came from God.

In fact, the idea of 'good' cannot have come to us from God. When we say 'God is good', that statement presupposes that we already have an idea of what 'good' means. God, we are saying, fits in with that idea. Thus, the very fact that we can describe God as good proves that we ourselves had the idea of 'good' and did not get it from God. Otherwise, our idea of 'good' would not be independent of God. 'Good' would be whatever God is. The statement that 'God is good' would mean nothing more than 'God is what God is'. And a statement like that would not help us very much in explaining how a sense of morality came to exist in this world.

Some of the things that God does in the Bible do strike us immediately as good (as when God sends an angel to stop Abraham killing his son, Genesis 22,11-13); some of the other things he does are not quite so obviously good (e.g. when he commands King Saul to go to the Amalekites and slaughter every man, woman, child, infant, ox, sheep, camel and ass that lives there, I Samuel 15,1-3). The fact that our moral sense tells us that some of God's deeds are good and others are not good proves that our moral sense is independent of God.

*If our concept of good came from God, then whatever God did would seem good to us. And if God were perfectly good, as Christians say, then the world he created would be perfectly good. But when we observe the world as it actually is, it does not always strike us as entirely perfect.*

\*     \*     \*

We are often invited to consider the good things in the world and see them as blessings conferred upon us by a good God. But then, in fairness, we should also consider the bad things.

44

We are told that God gave us life, which is a great good. But in that case he also gave us death, which is its opposite. Not only is dying usually unpleasant, but also many things in life itself are not good. Not everything that happens to us in life can be regarded as a blessing. But if we are to praise God for the good things in life, should we not also blame him for the bad?

*In 1938, when the Prime Minister, Mr Neville Chamberlain, returned from his meeting with Hitler at Munich with "peace in our time", the Archbishop of Canterbury described their agreement as "an answer to the great volume of prayer which has been rising to God" and he called upon Christians throughout the land to hold services of thanksgiving because the Lord had saved us, at the last moment, from the scourge of war. (The fact that he had not saved the Czechs was evidently not important). But a year later, when war broke out after all, the Archbishop did not call upon Christians throughout the land to meet in their churches and curse the Lord for changing his mind.*

One must conclude that Christians are apt to be selective about those things which they choose to attribute to the activity of God. It is only by such selectivity - by looking at the good things and refusing to see the rest - that they manage to sustain the idea that the world is governed by a God who is omnipotent, benevolent and good.

*     *     *

When we look at the world around us it does not seem to have been created according to moral principles. It makes little sense to say that nature is good.

Are the stars good? Is the spider good, when she eats her husband? Is the rain good, when it floods the valley? If the rain is good, why doesn't it fall when it is needed and stop when it will do harm? Why is it not always a blessing, rather than sometimes?

If nature were good, we might expect her to favour good things and destroy the bad. But fire from heaven has burnt York Minster as well as Sodom and Gomorrah. Good men fall ill and die of diseases just as readily as bad men. As a wise bard wrote at one of the high points of English literature,

The rain, it falleth on the just
And also on the unjust fellow
(Though mostly on the just, because
The unjust stole the just's umbrella).

Nature may seem both good and bad, or else neither good nor bad. The fact is, she has no moral sense at all.

Such ideas as good and bad arise in societies: when people live together they need to co-operate despite their conflicting desires and interests, and so they try to encourage some kinds of behaviour, which they call 'good', and discourage other kinds of behaviour, which they call 'bad'.

Aristotle pointed out that man is a 'social animal' (*zoon politikon*, in his language: the Greek word *politikon* means 'social'). Man is not the only social animal; many other animals also live together in groups, and even those which do not go about in flocks or herds usually live together in family groups, at least for a while, to bring up their young. In fact, all animals need to mate, and for that purpose they must acquire at least some basic minimum of social behaviour.

When animals live together, they have to behave according to some rules, so that they can rely on each other and trust each other. If the duck decided to eat up her ducklings instead of feeding and protecting them, then duck society would not last very long, and ducks would have died out long ago.

It is beneficial for any society if its members observe some rules of conduct which favour the society rather than themselves and so it is natural that societies always try to develop such rules and encourage the individual members of the society to conform to them.

Animals which live together in groups develop kinds of behaviour which benefit the group rather than the individual (e.g. when one rabbit warns the others of danger). In this way the notions of 'good' and 'bad', the moral ideas, are developed by societies to promote the interests of the group. They are patterns of social behaviour, not facts about the universe.

No social animal can afford to be completely selfish. It has to avoid actions that would harm the others on whom it depends, and it must do things that benefit the others. There has to be self-restraint, so that others are not threatened, and mutual aid, from which all members of the group may benefit. Young animals learn these social rules from their elders; they notice how the others behave and fall into line. It is basically the same with people, except that human society has become much more complicated. That is the origin of the ideas of 'good' and 'bad': as social life developed, it was necessary to develop rules for social behaviour, and we call those rules 'morality'.

Those rules are generally drummed into us by our elders at an early age and we are well aware of them; we are therefore immediately aware when our own behaviour offends against them or when the demands made upon us by some authority conflicts with the spirit of those rules and makes us rebel in the name of morality. What we call 'conscience' is our awareness of those rules, and conscience will quickly alert us when we are in conflict with them.

Societies and individual people may have different opinions about what those rules should be. People in different societies may also learn different moral codes and have differing views of what constitutes morality, and so their conscience may be sensitive to different things. Morality, for those who believe in God, may include their religious duty (so that failing to worship God or believe in him is 'immoral'); others may think it is more moral to have an open mind. But while societies may disagree over what they include in their idea of morality, there are no societies that have no moral values at all.

There is no evidence to suggest that societies where most citizens are very religious, such as Ireland or the Arab states, are more moral than those where most people are indifferent to religion. Has Iran become a better country since the Ayatollah and his mullahs came to power?

Acts of extreme cruelty are more common among peoples with a fervent religious belief, such as mediaeval Christian or modern Muslim societies (or their recent secular equivalent, the Fascist and Communist states), than in societies where most people are indifferent to such ideologies.

People who are fanatically committed to a particular belief usually have passionate and indignant feelings towards others who refuse to agree. That is why religious fanatics try to censor books or intimidate speakers and writers who do not agree with them, while people with no religion at all have no interest in trying to stop others from saying or writing whatever they like. We have seen this recently in the case of Salman Rushdie: even those Muslims who do not want to kill him still wish to see his book censored and suppressed, while non-believers prefer to allow free speech.

According to the Holy Koran, "The punishment of those who wage war against Allah and His Messenger . . . is execution, or crucifixion, or the cutting off of hands and feet from opposite sides, or exile from the land." (Koran, sura 5, verse 33). And, as we have recently seen, even to speak against this God may be regarded as an act of war. Is such an attitude morally superior to the tolerance of the atheist, who does not care about the glory of God, but usually does care about human beings?

Tolerance was the hope of the atheist Robert Ingersoll when he wrote: "This earth will be a paradise when men can, upon all these questions, differ, and yet grasp each other's hands as friends."

People who are convinced that God has given them the only true doctrine have no reason for tolerating other opinions which conflict with that doctrine. They can be quite sure that anyone who contradicts God's truth is a blasphemer against their God, and therefore God's enemy as well as their own. For that reason St Bernard of Clairvaux, as he preached the Second Crusade, declared that a person who kills an unbeliever does not commit homicide (killing a man) but malicide (killing an evil).

*As Voltaire said: "People who believe absurdities will commit atrocities."*

*      *      *

John Hick, in his *Arguments for the Existence of God* (pp. 59-67), draws attention to an important objection to the atheist's position which is seldom considered by atheist writers. Although he can explain the origin of social and moral behaviour, the atheist cannot claim that he is behaving rationally when he wilfully sacrifices himself for others.

Hick takes the hypothetical case of a young man who is willing to die for others: if the man is an atheist, then he believes there will be no heavenly or earthly reward, nothing of him will survive that might enjoy any future praise, and any momentary satisfaction of his sense that he is doing the right thing cannot outweigh the forty years or more of possibly happy life that he will lose. For the atheist it is "unreasonable for anything to be of more value to a man than his own existence . . . It follows that the act of self-destruction for the sake of mankind is not an act that can be rationally chosen or defended within the limits of the humanist conception of man." An atheist who sacrifices himself "is presupposing the falsity of his professed beliefs".

Hick's example is an extreme one, but the argument would apply equally in any case of genuine self-sacrifice, any wilful sacrifice of one's own true advantage. The argument rests upon an assumption that one's own survival is an absolute value. If you accept that premiss, then it follows that self-sacrifice must be irrational.

In Hick's example the Christian who sacrifices his own life for others is not behaving irrationally because he can expect a future reward, while for the atheist the same sacrifice would be real. If we follow that argument to its conclusion, and there is no good reason why we should not, then it would seem that moral behaviour, in the sense of wilfully sacrificing one's own advantage to that of others, is not possible for the Christian, since he expects a reward. In that case, only the atheist can be truly moral.

(If the Christian were to counter this by saying that he does the good for its own sake, not thinking of his future reward, then we could say that he has to suspend his Christian belief in order to be in a position to do a truly moral deed.)

But we may question the premiss of necessary egotism that lurks beneath this argument. Is it true that reason requires the preservation of the self, so that self-sacrifice must be irrational?

The function of reason is to help us draw true inferences from given premises. It tells us what will follow from the assumptions that we make. If I assume that the self is my highest good, then reason will tell me that self-sacrifice cannot be good. But reason cannot tell me whether I ought to put an absolute value upon my own existence. All that reason can ever do is provide me with true information by exposing falsehood.

Reason cannot tell me what I ought to desire. If I desire something, and propose to achieve it, then reason may guide me, but I must first have some desire or purpose. Hick argues that it is not rational to desire anything more than I desire my own survival. But desires are not prescribed by reason. They are a matter of personal taste.

If my supreme desire is to serve myself, then reason will advise me against altruism. But, as we have seen, the animal that I am is not an entirely selfish animal. My human nature, which determines my desires, is the nature of a social animal. I therefore quite naturally desire not only my own survival and well-being, but also that of others.

This is not pious nonsense, as any of us can tell by examining our own desires. All of us desire the welfare of others and we like to see other people happy. The whole world has rejoiced to see the peoples of eastern Europe obtain freedoms which we ourselves already had. We are angered by injustice, even when our own interests are not involved.

In any small child we can observe a natural impulse to help and to please. There are, of course, other impulses, and children can also be very selfish. But the fact remains: our desire to serve ourselves is not absolute. We have both selfish and unselfish desires. When we see someone in trouble, we immediately want to help. If we apply reason to guide us then our conduct will be equally rational, whether or not the goal is a selfish one.

*Altruism is just as natural as selfishness, and we can be rational in serving the interests of others just as well as in serving ourselves.*

## The Consensus of Opinion

The 'proofs' of God's existence which we have considered do not look very convincing. There are others, but they are either variations on these, or else so weak that even believers have generally preferred to ignore them. When you consider that these proofs represent the best that could be done by the best philosophers in the world for more than two thousand years, it really does begin to look as if there just isn't any better proof. If one could be found, then surely somebody by now would have found it. And if Christians had ever found a good proof, then surely they would use it.

*If God had been supporting his defenders, as they believed he was, then he might perhaps have warned them that the argu-*

51

*ments they were putting forward to prove his existence would not*
*stand up to scrutiny.* *It seems he did not.*

*      *      *

But we would be wrong to refuse to believe everything which we cannot prove. In practice, we regularly believe many things we cannot prove.

I believe in the existence of icebergs in the North Atlantic, though I have never seen one and have no way of proving that they exist.

My belief in icebergs, however, is not irrational. Though I cannot prove their existence, I do have very good reasons for believing in them. My main reason is the consensus of opinion. My belief in icebergs is supported by an enormous number of reliable and independent witnesses who have no motive whatever for wishing to deceive me (among them all the writers of standard reference books); the testimony of those witnesses has been checked many times by competent authorities who are in a position to know the facts. Since those authorities are well informed and have every reason to tell the truth, it is reasonable for me to trust their word.

I also have no good reason to disbelieve them, since what they tell me about icebergs does not conflict with the rest of my knowledge of the world I live in. Icebergs fit in with my general view of the way the world works, a view I have derived from all kinds of different sources, including my own experience. It is therefore far more likely that icebergs really do exist than that all these sources have misled me. And so, although I have no proof, my belief in their existence is perfectly rational.

Could it be the same with God? The 'proofs' of his existence are clearly inadequate; but is there a consensus of opinion which it would be reasonable for us to join?

Many, if not most Protestant theologians today agree that the old 'proofs' of God's existence are not valid and do not work. But

52

they still believe, and most of them are satisfied that their belief is rational. One reason is that they share their belief with many others.

There are indeed many who say that God exists. Are those people really in a position to know? Can we trust them? Does their testimony fit in with the rest of our view of the world, so that we have no reason to disbelieve them? If so, it will be rational for us to believe in God, even though we have no proof.

*　　　*　　　*

Millions believe; but, as we have seen, the number is not important. There are also millions who disbelieve, and the believers could be wrong. Indeed, most of them *must* be wrong, because they believe so many different things that the 'God' they believe in is not the same God.

*This point has been illustrated by Sir Hermann Bondi. Suppose, he says, three different witnesses testify that they have seen an accident. One of them says the car he saw was blue and heading north; another says it was grey and heading east; the third says it was yellow and going south. Would we conclude: 'at least we are sure of one thing; it was a car and not a motorbike!'?*

*It is more likely that we would conclude that such witnesses are unreliable and we should refuse to believe any of them. When witnesses contradict each other it is not reasonable to assume that any point they happen to agree on must be true; their contradiction does not strengthen their case, even where they agree, but discredits it.*

*It is the same when various groups of believers tell us contradictory things about God.*

*When the conceptions of God are in contradiction, any reason we may find for believing in one God is also a reason for not believing in another. The number of conflicting Gods does not enable us to say, "Well, at least we can agree there is some kind of God" ; instead, it discredits them all and makes us doubt whether any of them can really be true.*

*       *       *

Millions believe, but most of them are merely accepting what they once were told. They believe a tradition that was handed down to them. Before we can believe what they believe we need to look at that tradition. Is it reliable? Were the original writers of the tradition people we can trust? Were they in a position to know the truth, and have they written what they knew fairly and impartially?

Traditions about God have been handed down in writings which report how God revealed himself to men. That is true of the Christian Bible, which bears witness to God and to Jesus. The Bible is not so much a book as a large collection of books, some of them written originally in Hebrew and others in Greek over a period of some 800 years, from about 600 BC to AD 200. Our problem is: can we believe what those ancient writers tell us?

In order to judge whether we can safely trust their tradition we should need to examine the contents of those books and consider how they came to be written down and put together. I have done this in a companion to this book called *What is the Bible?* (obtainable from the Rationalist Press Association) and so I will not go into it again in any detail here. The briefest outline will suffice.

The Bible's writers record events that had happened long before their own time. The early books about God's relationship with Moses were written hundreds of years after Moses had died, while the gospels, which tell the story of Jesus, were written some fifty years or more after the death of Jesus. The writers therefore could not possibly have witnessed for themselves the events which they record: their testimony consists of what they were told, or copied, or invented. They certainly believed in God and they had heard about his actions in the history of their people, but we cannot reasonably say that they themselves were in a position to know.

(Some Christians say that God inspired those writers and spoke through them, so that they could write down things which they would not naturally have known. But this is simply a hypothesis, like the hypothesis of God. Those who believe such an extraordinary idea would need to produce satisfactory evidence to substantiate it before they could expect us to take it seriously. They would also have to explain the contradictions in the Bible, which should not have arisen if the writers were all inspired by the same God.)

Not only did the writers live long after the events, so that they could not have witnessed them themselves, but most of them were also propagandists, if not religious fanatics. Their reason for writing was not to record facts but to win support for their cause. Far from being impartial, they are well known to have been very biased, as Christian theologians have proved and readily agree. They are certainly not the sort of people whom we would normally trust, since we know very well that it was not their intention to write an impartial report.

In any case, the 'God' whom they describe (especially in the Old Testament) is very different from the sort of 'God' who is used by some modern religious thinkers to explain the existence of the world. The Bible's 'God' is very much a person, a kind of superhuman person with a strong will and human passions, a person with a desire for praise and a taste for sacrifices, who directs the history of his own chosen people, the people of Israel. He changes in the later parts of the Bible into a more vague and mysterious God of love, who cares for all people, not only the Jews, and who sent his son down to earth. If we wish to believe in some modern philosophical concept of God then we certainly cannot quote the Bible as evidence for his existence, because the God whom the Bible bears witness to is quite different.

Believers, at different times, have had different ideas of God, and so if you examine the Bible and show that its idea of 'God' does not make sense, many Christians will say that they now believe in yet another, less personal kind of God. Even within the Bible we can see that the idea of God is changing from the early books to the later ones. In the course of time, the colourful, very personal God of the Jews, who was originally the war god called Yahweh or Jehovah, became more vague and general, so that it became less easy to show that he does not exist.

That process has gone on especially in the last hundred years or so. The God our great-grandparents believed in was still very much a person with strong passions, who watched us and punished us for our sins; but modern Christians often like to forget God's personal features, such as his anger, and think of him in more vague and abstract terms. Professor Flew has illustrated this by quoting a story first told by the philosopher John Wisdom:

*"Once upon a time two explorers came upon a clearing in the jungle. In the clearing were growing many flowers and many weeds. One explorer says, 'Some gardener must tend this plot'. The other disagrees, 'There is no gardener'. So they pitch their tents and set a watch. No gardener is ever seen. 'But perhaps he is an invisible gardener.' So they set up a barbed-wire fence. They electrify it. They patrol with bloodhounds. (For they remember how H. G. Wells's Invisible Man could be smelt and touched though he could not be seen.) But no shrieks ever suggest that some intruder has received a shock. No movements of the wire ever betray an invisible climber. The bloodhounds never give cry. Yet still the Believer is not convinced. 'But there is a gardener, invisible, intangible, insensible to electric shocks, a gardener who has no scent and makes no sound, a gardener who comes secretly to look after the garden which he loves.' At last the Sceptic despairs, 'But what remains of your original assertion? Just how does what you call an invisible, intangible,*

56

*eternally elusive gardener differ from an imaginary gardener or
even from no gardener at all?'"*

Thus the idea of God, which in the first books of the Bible has a
very clear and definite meaning, becomes more and more vague
until, in the minds of some modern believers, little is left beyond
an empty word. This is what philosophers call the 'death by a
thousand qualifications' - the idea has become so much qualified
that it has lost its original meaning.

It may seem remarkable that people should stick to an old
belief after it has lost its meaning. But that is often the case with
religious beliefs. G. A. Wells, in his book *Religious Postures* (p.
65), writes of a famous theologian that "he was unwilling to
relinquish his conclusions, but had some difficulty in finding
plausible premisses". That happens because the emotional appeal of religious belief is very strong. People will therefore cling
fervently to their belief, not only when they cannot find credible
grounds to justify it rationally, but even when they are no longer
able to understand and state clearly what it is that they say they
believe.

Historians, psychologists and anthropologists may help us
to understand why people are so keen to believe that there is a
God. That idea (if they can believe in it) gives them hope and
comfort, and it seems to give a purpose to their lives. A shared
belief will help a society to hold firmly together, making it easier
for its members to agree and collaborate against a common
enemy. Fear of God also may help people to unite, as well as
encouraging them to obey the rules of their leaders (especially
the priests).

But to understand the reasons why other people believe
cannot in any way persuade us that what they believe is true. In
fact, when we see that the belief of others is likely to be based on
something other than reason we may be still more inclined to
conclude that the belief of others is not a reason why we
ourselves should believe.

*I believe in the existence of icebergs because the people who have written about them were in a position to know the facts; they had good reasons for reporting the facts objectively and no reason at all for wishing to persuade or mislead me. They were not likely to be fanatics and they had no particular axe to grind. What they wrote can be checked by others, who also have no reason for any bias. And, most important: what they have written about icebergs fits in with everything else I know about the world, so that I have no reason to disbelieve it.*

*None of this can be said of the Bible traditions about God.*

## Personal Experience of God

Not everything we believe has been urged upon us, either by reason or by the consensus of opinion around us. Most commonly we believe things because we have seen or felt them, that is, we trust our own experience and our own feelings rather than rational arguments. We believe that the world exists, not because we are persuaded by some argument, but because we have experienced the world. Perhaps it is the same with God. We cannot see God, but many of those who believe in him tell us that they have had personal experience of his existence. Is it really possible that they may have experienced him in some way, and is it reasonable for us to trust what they say they have experienced? That is something which we must now consider.

*       *       *

Many believers say that they have experienced God in their own lives. "I have felt the presence of God", they say, or "God has spoken to me."

You cannot get inside another person and know for yourself what he has felt. At the same time you are not convinced when he says he can feel, or in some other way experience something which you do not experience. If your friend says he can see a cat on the wall, and you do not see it, then you won't believe the cat is really there. You will believe he is seeing things.

Perhaps your friend really does experience something which you can't experience. That will happen, for example, if he has a headache. But you can remember having experienced headaches in the past, so you can agree that what he says is likely to be true - and anyway it does not conflict with what you otherwise know about the world. In such a case you have no reason to doubt what he tells you.

But if your friend tells you that he can experience something that is very unlikely to be true, then it is sensible for you not to believe him. When I tell you that I have seen a cow eating grass, then it is reasonable for you to believe me. But when I tell you that I have seen a cow jumping over the moon, it is reasonable for you not to believe me. You may allow that I did see something, but it was not really a cow jumping over the moon. Although you cannot know my experience in either case, you can judge whether what I say I experienced is likely or not.

The experience of God's presence is not an ordinary thing, like cows eating grass; it is extraordinary, like cows jumping over moons. That is a very good reason indeed for believing that what your friend tells you he has experienced was not really the presence of God.

Things that people say they have experienced are not always what they seem to be. For one thing, it is possible to have hallucinations. Drugs can produce vivid hallucinations, and the experiences which follow are very real to the people who have them. People may also 'see things' when they are very upset, or when they are starved of food (for example, the saints, who kept having visions of God, used to fast for very long periods; and most religions encourage fasting). People who say they have personally experienced God are often emotional people who might be expected to have intense feelings.

Another factor is 'wishful thinking'. People who experience God are usually people who already believed in God, or who are trying very hard to make themselves believe. They hope that God exists. They would like religion to be true, so they persuade themselves that it really is. Then they start to feel it is true deep inside themselves. And they experience the presence of God.

The process is not always deliberate: it may be unconscious. But that does not make it any less real.

Usually, when you experience something, other people can also experience it. When they can't, there is at least some reason to wonder whether that person's feeling is to be trusted. Perhaps your friend really does experience something. But how can you know it is God?

Is it likely that some people experience God and others do not? If the presence of God is really there to be experienced, why do most people not notice it? You would think that God would give the religious sense to everybody, so that we could all experience his presence and hear what he says, rather than allow only some of us to experience him. Why should he wish to keep his existence a secret from the rest of us?

People of different religious faiths often say they have experiences of God, but those experiences very often do not agree with each other. When God is experienced by Hindu believers he may be Krishna or Shiva, the God whom Muslims experience is Allah, and the Christian God only shows himself to Christian believers.

Even if you say that it is the same God whom the Muslims experience as Allah, the Christians as Jesus, and so on, it is still hard to explain why this God says quite different things to Muslims and to Christians. At one time he used to tell Christians that they should burn witches and start wars against Muslims; he tells Muslims not to eat pork and he tells Hindus not to hurt cattle. God was always appearing to the saints and the prophets and telling them things which nobody would believe today. Are you going to say that the personal experience of God which the saint and the crusader and the witch-hunter had was not real, while the experience of God which some people today say they have is real? Why?

The man who says he has experienced God already had the idea of God in his mind. When he felt a deep emotion, he assumed it was the presence of God. Another man who had the same kind of experience might have called it 'awe', 'ecstasy', or something else. It might be the kind of excitement you feel when you are stimulated by poetry or music; you may have felt something like it when looking at a landscape, or at the stars, or in contemplating the size of the universe or the wonders of nature. All the believer can really say is that he felt something and he thought it was the presence of God. What he calls an experience of God is really his own interpretation of some experience.

A research group founded at Oxford University in 1969 collected details of religious experiences which people said they had had, so that they could be studied properly. And, apart from noticing that many of the people who had these experiences were, to say the least, rather odd, they came up against another problem: some of the things they experienced did not agree with their religion. A lady said she had seen her dog in heaven. But Christians are not supposed to believe that dogs have souls and go to heaven. Is it likely that she really saw her dog in heaven? Or would it be more reasonable to believe that the lady was so upset when her dog died that she imagined very strongly that she had seen him in heaven?

*Another thing which the research showed was that about one third of the people studied appeared to have had a 'religious experience'. That implies that the other two thirds had not (a point not stressed in their report). But if religious experiences are real, why don't we all have them? Could it be that all of us are sensitive to feelings and experiences and one third of the people asked thought that the experiences which they had were religious?*

# Occam's Razor

All of us have experiences, of one kind or another, and we need hypotheses to explain them. That is how the hypothesis of the existence of gods arose in the first place. Our early ancestors experienced many things which they could not understand, and for them it seemed likely that there must be gods, or other unseen beings, causing these things to happen.

But as we gained a better understanding of the processes of nature we found it easier to use other hypotheses, for which there was better evidence. At one time a thunderstorm was best explained by assuming that the thunder god was angry; but now we understand something of meteorology and find it easier to explain such things without a thunder god. Our scientific explanations fit in with the rest of our knowledge about nature, while the thunder god does not. In this way the hypothesis of gods became superfluous.

For a long time 'God' was preserved to explain the things that still could not be explained by science: in this function he was known as the 'God of the gaps': his job was to fill the gaps in our scientific knowledge. But, as more and more of those gaps were plugged, 'God' became more and more unemployed. Religion was retreating as knowledge advanced. With every gap that was filled this God became less credible and so the whole idea of a 'God of the gaps' was discredited. He was becoming a superfluous hypothesis, because things could be explained better without him.

Of course it is still *possible* that there is a God who accounts for those things which science cannot yet explain. But such a hypothesis rests upon nothing at all except ignorance. It is like the idea that, because we cannot see God in any part of the sky which we can observe, he must therefore exist in some place that our telescopes cannot reach. It is, as Einstein wrote, "a doctrine which is able to maintain itself not in clear light, but only in the dark". The things which we can observe in nature do not justify belief in God, because they can be accounted for by simpler hypotheses; we have no ground for assuming that God is justified by those things which we cannot observe.

*    *    *

It is perfectly rational for us to invent some hypothesis to explain the things which we see around us. But it is rational only if the hypothesis we invent is necessary. It is a well-known rule of logical thinking that we must always prefer the simplest hypothesis which accounts for all the observed facts. This rule, that "hypotheses must not be multiplied", was taught in the Middle Ages by the philosopher William of Occam and is known, after him, as 'Occam's Razor'. The hypothesis which accounts most economically for all the known facts is justified by those facts; but any complication to that hypothesis, any additional hypothesis which is not required by those facts, is arbitrary and therefore not justified.

To put it in plainer language: it is not reasonable to prefer a complicated explanation to a simpler one.

*If my dog comes into the house soaking wet, the simplest hypothesis for me - living in the west of Wales - is that it is raining. That is the explanation that usually proves correct. It is possible, of course, that in this particular case the simple explanation might be wrong - perhaps the dog fell into a river, perhaps somebody who doesn't like dogs has thrown a bucket of water over him. But, as long as I have no special evidence to support any of these less likely explanations, as long as the easy hypothesis of 'rain as usual' will equally well explain what I have seen, then the reasonable thing for me to do is to prefer it to any of the more complicated ones.*

63

*Since I have a perfectly adequate natural explanation to account for the observed fact, it would be quite unreasonable for me to seek a supernatural one, for example, to suppose that a god or a devil must have made the dog wet.*

\*       \*       \*

In the last century scientists used to believe that space was filled with a substance which they called 'ether'. That hypothesis was the best way to explain how light-waves were carried to us from the sun. But when people found better ways of explaining the transmission of light, the idea of 'ether' became a superfluous hypothesis, and it fell a victim to the logical law of 'Occam's Razor'. It no longer explained anything, and so scientists stopped believing in it. That is how it is with the idea of 'God'. What we see in nature can now be explained more economically without the idea of 'God'. We cannot, of course, explain everything, but the 'God' hypothesis does not make our explaining any easier. So it no longer makes any sense to believe in that idea. The hypothesis has now lost its purpose.

The function of a hypothesis is to explain things we do not understand in terms of what we know. It makes little sense to do the reverse: to explain nature, which increasingly is becoming known and understood, in terms of a God whom we do not know and understand.

In the case of the God hypothesis, the known facts - the existence and behaviour of the world as we know it - can be largely explained by the various hypotheses of natural science and philosophy. They cannot be explained any better by adding the hypothesis of a 'Creator'. The God hypothesis is therefore a needless complication not justified by the observed facts. It is ruled out by Occam's Razor.

*Do not multiply hypotheses!*

# What difference would it make?

If somebody says in a court of law that a certain thing happened, then he must produce evidence to support his claim. If his evidence is not adequate, the court will not believe him. The court will judge that it is not reasonable to believe him because he cannot support what he says. Therefore, if someone claims you did something there is a 'presumption of innocence' which stands until the person who makes his claim produces sufficient evidence to show that what he says is true.

This rule of evidence applies equally when somebody claims that God exists. The person who makes that claim must produce his evidence that what he says is true. If his evidence is inadequate or unsatisfactory, then we shall not believe him. There is no need for the sceptic to try to prove God's non-existence; it is up to the person who says he exists to provide satisfactory reasons to support his assertion and show that it is likely to be true. Professor Flew makes this point very lucidly in his book *The Presumption of Atheism* (1976).

I do not believe that there are small furry wombles on Wimbledon Common. I do not have any proof that these animals do not exist, and I do not need any. It is reasonable for me not to believe until somebody who claims it is true comes along and produces sufficient evidence to support his case.

Usually, the religious believer is not at all keen to produce his evidence. He tells you to 'have faith', and if you will not he may say you are short-sighted, or materialistic, or arrogant, or simple, naive and unimaginative, and perhaps in some way immoral, and he will not like your attitude. If he takes that line you can be pretty sure he has no credible evidence to support his case and he is looking for an easy way out that will save him from thinking. But that will not change the basic law of rational debate: he who makes the claim must produce the evidence.

A fair and proper way to press the believer to produce his evidence is to ask: 'How would the world be different if God did not exist?'

The whole of nature appears to function just as if there were no God at all. The universe does not seem to be good or bad, it neither loves us nor hates us, its behaviour seems to obey impersonal natural patterns rather than a personal will or a divine law. We see no evidence of any supernatural interventions, such as miracles. We never see God or hear him, if we speak or pray to him he does not appear to answer, and we see no consequences of his existence in the world around us and the way the world runs. But if neither our reason nor our senses give us any evidence that he exists, if we are not able to see or feel either him or what he is doing, then we have no reason to believe in him at all. The 'presumption of atheism' must apply.

The only way we can ever know anything at all is by using our own minds and drawing conclusions from what we see and experience of the world around us. Since we do not see or feel God, and never witness him doing anything at all, our experience gives us no ground for thinking that he exists. If he did exist, he must be keeping his existence so secret that no reasonable person could believe in him. Why should he do that?

Some Christians argue that if God were to speak clearly and reveal himself, then we would have no real freedom of choice. We would then have to believe in him. Therefore God remains mysterious, so that we are free to decide for ourselves whether to believe and be 'saved'.

Apart from the fact that this contradicts parts of the Bible, where God does reveal himself plainly to some people (using miracles to convince them) and where it is stated that God himself determines who will believe and be saved (Matthew 22,14; Luke 13,24-27; John 6,44; 13,18; Romans 8,29; 9,18), it also is not a valid argument. However plainly God were to reveal himself, we still should have to choose whether or not to believe his revelation: it would merely be more rational for us to choose belief, because we should then have substantial evidence to support belief. Our belief would then be justified, and not arbitrary.

We have to choose anyway, whether or not we have adequate evidence, but in the absence of adequate evidence it is more rational for us to choose not to believe.

It is hardly likely that God exists but wants us to believe in him irrationally. If that were so, why did he give us the faculty of reason?

If the atheist were to meet God in all his glory, or witness God's reaction to prayer, or to see God's interventions in nature, or observe that nature obeys a good and merciful will, then he would have to admit that he was wrong. But those things do not actually happen.

And so he may fairly say to the believer: 'What sort of things would have to happen, or not happen, to convince you that you are wrong? What would you expect the world to be like if God did not exist?'

If he has no coherent answer, then he is going to believe anyway, and there is nothing that will change his mind. He will simply appeal to faith, and he will believe regardless of the evidence. When somebody takes that view there is no point in arguing with him, because he has placed himself beyond the reach of reason.

*"To offer reasons to a bigot is like offering medicine to a dead man", wrote Thomas Paine.*

Remember: when somebody says that he believes in some theory, ask him to predict what consequences of that theory we shall observe if the theory is true, and to say what sort of evidence would convince him that the theory is wrong.

# Other Reasons for Belief

People first believed in gods because that hypothesis helped them to understand the hidden processes of nature and gave them hope that, by pleasing the gods, they might be able to obtain favours from them and influence the course of events. Thus they began to deal with the gods as they dealt with other people.

Their belief, of course, was not merely practical. They also feared the gods and needed to appease them. They feared many unseen powers in nature. Life was short and dangerous, death and disease could strike at any moment and human beings were helpless against strange forces that seemed to rule the world, a world which they made still more terrible by the creatures of their own superstition.

They could not have conceived the world around them in terms of matter and energy: they assumed the world was alive, like themselves. Their attitude has been described imaginatively and vividly by Winwood Reade in *The Martyrdom of Man* (1872):

"To those primeval people the sun was a great being, who brightened them in his pleasure, and who scorched them in his wrath. The earth was a sleeping monster: sometimes it rose a little and turned itself in bed. They walked upon its back when living; they were put into its belly when they died. Fire was a savage animal, which bit when it was touched. The birds and beasts were foreigners, possessing languages and customs of their own. The plants were dumb creatures, with characters good or bad, sometimes gloomy in aspect, malignant in their fruit, sometimes dispensing wholesome food and pleasant shade. These various forms of nature they treated precisely as if they had been men."

They feared demons, evil spirits, and the ghosts of the dead, who must surely still live in some unknown form and might do them harm. Against all such things they sought the help of gods and did what they could, with worship, prayer and sacrifice, to make them friendly. Thus religion was born of fear.

As small communities joined to form nations and empires, local gods were often subordinated to some great tribal god and might one day be forgotten. The Jews reduced the number of the gods to one, who eventually became universal, but still they regarded him as a person who liked to receive praise and sacrifices. In due course he became the God of the Christians and then of the Muslims, and still he remains a personal God.

When the Bible says that God made man in his own image, we can be sure that the reverse is true. People liked to imagine God as a person like themselves, so that they might hope to understand and communicate with him. We all like to assume that others are like ourselves, and the personal analogy applied equally to human ideas of God.

*In the 5th century BC Xenophanes observed: "The Ethiopians say their gods are snub-nosed and black, the Thracians that theirs have light blue eyes and red hair."*

*More recently, Bertrand Russell noted that in Haiti the images of God are black, while those of Satan are white.*

*The French writer Montesquieu (1689-1755) remarked that if triangles worshipped a god he would have three sides.*

In a poem which develops the same idea Rupert Brooke considers - in a way which is both comic and serious - what sort of a God it may be that fishes dream of:

> "... somewhere, beyond Space and Time,
> Is wetter water, slimier slime!
> And there (they trust) there swimmeth One
> Who swam ere rivers were begun,
> Immense, of fishy form and mind,
> Squamous, omnipotent and kind;
> And under that Almighty Fin,
> The littlest fish may enter in."

In the Christian culture God is traditionally masculine; he is 'Our Father'. Sigmund Freud, who did not himself believe in God, explained him in psychological terms as a father-figure to whom young children turn when they discover that their own father is not absolutely powerful and good. As with many of Freud's ideas, that is not likely to be the whole truth, and the 'father' factor may be still less important today when human fathers are nothing like omnipotent; but the wish to have a strong protector and 'father' to rely on may still make people wish to believe that God exists, especially if they are young or insecure.

The idea that God is a person, whose 'image' is like that of a man, must now seem remarkably improbable; yet that is very plainly the way he is represented in the whole Christian tradition, and the idea retains its appeal because we find it easier to understand and relate to God if we imagine him as a person.

*      *      *

One of the oldest reasons for believing in gods was the need to explain miracles, which at one time seem to have occurred in great numbers. If they are now less frequent, that is partly because we now understand such things as eclipses of the sun and no longer see them as miracles, and partly because we are not so inclined to believe all the tall stories we are told. When Mr Elvis Presley is reported as being seen alive and well in a hamburger bar at Kalamazoo, Michigan, twelve years after his death, some of us are apt to be sceptical; but such scepticism was not common at the time when Jesus allegedly appeared to his disciples.

When Hume criticised the belief in miracles in the 18th century he noted that miracles are frequent "among ignorant and barbarous nations" and when they are believed by civilised peoples they are found to have come from "ignorant and barbarous ancestors", whose stories are still accepted because they now have the authority of tradition.

When the gospels present the credentials of Jesus they stress more than anything else the many miracles he performed, calling them 'signs' which show that he truly was the son of God. The

Christian religion was originally founded upon the belief in such miracles as the incarnation and resurrection of Jesus and on the many miracles which he, and after him his apostles and saints performed. All saints, in order to be recognised by the Catholic Church, must have performed at least two proper miracles, and most of them performed many more. The Catholic Church has holy places, such as Lourdes, Knock and Fatima, where people go by thousands to witness miracles today.

But Hume, more than anyone else, has made it impossible for most of us now to believe in any miracles at all. He showed not only that religions contradict each other, so that the miracles which 'prove' one God must disprove another, but that miracles are in principle very unlikely. We recognise that a miracle has occurred only when the ordinary course of events, which accords with what we call the 'laws' of nature, has been suspended. Without that there is no miracle.

But when someone tells us that this has happened, it is always more likely that he is mistaken, or lying, than that nature's course really was suspended, because we have more evidence that people can be mistaken, or lie, than that the laws of nature ever were suspended. All our past observations are evidence in favour of the regular patterns of nature; so much evidence must outweigh the evidence in favour of any miracle, which is merely that somebody said it happened. Therefore, "no testimony is sufficient to establish a miracle, unless the testimony be of such a kind, that its falsity would be more miraculous, than the fact, which it endeavours to establish".

*In the blunter, but less precise formulation of Thomas Paine:*
*"Is it more probable that nature should go out of her course, or that a man should tell a lie?"*

Like the other 'proofs' of God's existence, the evidence of his miracles is no longer considered satisfactory; but, when an event occurs that is hard to explain, many believers, and not only

71

at Lourdes, Knock and Fatima, are still glad to use the report of an unexplained event as welcome evidence supporting their case.

*       *       *

Another reason for believing in God is that, without him, there would be no purpose in the existence of the world, or in our own lives. God, we are told, created the world deliberately, which means he did it for some purpose. It continues to exist because "God is working his purpose out". This gives a sense to all history: it is leading somewhere. And since my own life, too, was deliberately created by God, it also has a purpose. There is a meaning to my life.

This argument, however, is not evidence. What it comes to is this: It would be nice to think the world was made deliberately and we are here for some purpose; therefore it was and we are. Expressed in plain terms, the fallacy is obvious. The fact that something would be nice does not in any way help us prove that it is really the case.

Such animals as ourselves often do things for some purpose, and so it appeals to us to think that the whole cosmos was made for a purpose; but we see no reliable evidence of any purpose in the universe. Similarly, it would be nice to think that I myself am here for a purpose, rather than by accident. But I see no evidence that it is really the case.

If I was placed here for a purpose, must not also every bird, every worm, every tree and every blade of grass have been placed here for a purpose? How can I argue that my life has a purpose, but theirs has not? And if a blade of grass in the field just happened to grow because the seed fell there and the conditions were right, then is it not the same with the tree, the worm, the bird — and me?

When we look back down the course of history it is easy to imagine, rather egotistically, that it was all meant to lead up to us. But any other life-form that happened to develop would feel just the same when it looked back: all history leads up to the present. The way we have come must necessarily lead to where we are now. But that does not prove that we came that way on purpose, or that some purpose outside ourselves has been guiding our steps. If there were a purpose, we should expect it to continue into the future; but when we look forward instead of back, the illusion of purpose and direction will disappear at once.

*A purpose cannot exist by itself: it presupposes some intelligent being that intends to do something. If the universe existed for a purpose, that would imply there was some being, such as a god, from whom that purpose came. What about ourselves? If there is no God, does it follow that our lives have no purpose?*

No, it does not follow, because human beings are intelligent life forms and we ourselves can have purposes. It may be that no god gave us any purpose, but that does not stop us from finding a purpose for ourselves and in that way giving a meaning to life.

We can all think of people who lived purposeful lives. Among them there are many sceptics and atheists; they include Charles Darwin, whose purpose was to discover the laws of evolution, and Henri Dunant, who founded the International Red Cross. Julian Huxley was the first Director-General of UNESCO, Brock Chisholm the first Director-General of the World Health Organisation, Gilbert Murray helped to found the League of Nations. Einstein and Freud were Honorary Associates of the Rationalist Press Association; so was Lord Boyd-Orr, who devoted his life to improving the state of agriculture in the Third World. Nobody could say that these people had no meaning to their lives, or they lived without purpose. What is more, the purpose of their lives was a purpose they had chosen for themselves, not one that had been imposed upon them. They did not live their lives to serve the purpose of a god, but dedicated themselves to a purpose freely chosen.

We do not, of course, have to limit ourselves to a single purpose. Most of us find a number of different purposes which give meaning to our lives. It is probably the case that those people who can find in this way some purpose in life, a reason for living which is greater than satisfying their own needs, enjoy a more fulfilled and satisfying quality of life than those who do not. They know where they are going, or at least trying to go, and a purpose outside themselves will unite them with others, while selfishness will cut them off from others.

The argument that we need the hypothesis of God in order to have a purpose fails, then, on two counts. Firstly, God would not really exist just because we want to have a purpose to our lives. And secondly, we can very well have a purpose to our lives without any God; in fact it is only when we have no God that the purpose to our lives becomes our own.

*      *      *

We have already considered the argument that there must be a God because we have a moral sense, and we have seen that it is not valid. The same kind of argument is also used in another form: the belief in God teaches us morality, and so it is necessary for society that citizens should believe in God.

This, like the argument that we must believe in order to make our life meaningful, is really not evidence at all but an appeal to expediency. It expects us to believe in God because our belief would be useful to society, not because it is true. It is like the attitude of those parents who wish their children to be brought up as Christians, not because they believe that Christianity is true, but because they think it is a good thing. But even if believing in God did make us more moral, that would not make God really exist.

Anyway, is it true that people who believe are more moral than those who do not?

74

If we are not able to answer that question from our own personal experience, then we may look back into those periods in history when religious belief was intense and universal, such as the Dark Ages and the Middle Ages. Are those times noted for the moral behaviour of the people and the good order of society? Or do we remember them as a period of cruelty and persecution, the age of crusades and inquisitions, heresy trials, witch-hunts, judicial torture and public executions?

Christian leaders today are no longer so bloodthirsty as their predecessors were in the Age of Faith. Is that because the Bible which they follow now contains more humanity than it used to contain? Or is it because, in the last few centuries, a new secular and scientific culture has grown up, which Christian leaders at first resisted, but eventually had to accept? Is it because their congregations have become better informed and better educated, so that they have stopped being afraid of almighty God and the unspeakable tortures of his hell, and have learnt to care instead for the health and happiness of human beings?

If 'morality' means having faith, then people who believe must, by definition, be more moral than those who do not. But the atheist will argue that when faith expects a man to say what he does not really believe, or to make himself believe things which his own mind tells him are not true, then this faith is likely to have an adverse effect on his moral character rather than improve it.

A number of independent surveys, conducted both in Britain and abroad, have shown that Roman Catholic schools produce a significantly higher proportion of delinquents than other schools and that the proportion of Catholics in prisons is two to three times higher than in the population as a whole. In Britain the pattern is that Catholics make up about a tenth of the general population but a quarter of the prison population. Such figures do not support the opinion that a religious education is good for the moral standards of society.

The 'moral' argument, like the 'purpose' argument, has two answers. Firstly, even if belief did make us more moral, that would not help to prove that God exists. And secondly, there is no evidence to show that believing really does make people more moral.

*       *       *

One reason for thinking it is good for other people to believe in God is the hope that believing in God will help the poor to accept the unpleasant conditions of their life in this world and prevent them from rebelling. That is why Karl Marx called religion the "opium of the people".

This, too, is nothing like a proof but an appeal to expediency: it is useful for the state if the people believe. Perhaps, rather than hope that believing in a happy afterlife with God will help the people to endure their oppression, we should stop oppressing them. That is what Karl Marx meant.

In past centuries the vast majority of people suffered extreme poverty and misery. They had to struggle hard for mere survival and had no chance of living their lives in security, comfort and happiness. The promise of happiness in another life helped them to endure their present misery.

But now things are different, and most people do have a real chance of happiness in this life. Instead of worshipping and glorifying God, as Christian society had always done, the atheist Jeremy Bentham sought to promote "the greatest happiness of the greatest number". If society will adopt that ideal, then people may now be able to enjoy real happiness in this world, rather than live this earthly life in misery, hoping for happiness afterwards — only to be cheated of that happiness when death turns out to be genuine after all.

When we consider how most people in all past ages have believed, we should not forget the dreadful conditions of life in

76

all past ages, which made those people want to believe. Even today, belief is still deeply entrenched and virtually universal in the poorest countries.

*Religious belief is now out of date for intellectual reasons: science has taught us a view of the world which makes much better sense. But belief is also out of date for social reasons: the pain and poverty which made life unbearable for most people without the comfort of religion are at last being overcome so that humanity can hope for a better life in the future.*

# Is the idea plausible?

At one time, when man seemed to be raised high up above the animal kingdom and this world of ours was thought to be the centre of the universe, it may have seemed plausible to believe that a good God had created it, together with the sun and stars to give us warmth and light. God created this world for the sake of man, who was lord over all the animals, he guided man's history with a benevolent hand and his main concern was for man's moral conduct and his future salvation.

But nowadays we recognise that man is an animal, like the others, and closely related to them, indeed the human species has only appeared quite recently, and this world is just a minor planet circling a not very remarkable sun somewhere on the edge of one among billions of galaxies. It is hard now to go on believing that man's salvation was God's reason for creating so vast a universe, and that all the stars were made in order to light up this earth, as we are told in the book of Genesis. Our expanding horizons have put man into his place - a very humble place in the vast scheme of things - and in so doing they also have made it highly unlikely that all these things were created by a God who made man in his own image and whose purpose was the eternal bliss of those men who believed in him.

In the last two or three centuries enormous progress has been made in explaining the nature of the world around us. As more and more things have been explained and understood without the hypothesis of God, the atheist's position has been getting stronger and stronger; at the same time, the Christian position has been getting weaker and weaker as there are fewer things left for his God to explain.

Now that we understand how very tiny this world is in a vast universe, how very long it existed before we came into being, how closely we are related to the apes, and how much of our behaviour can be explained by conditioning rather than free will, the idea of God has become far less plausible than it was before. Alex Carey expressed the point in language that is challenging and yet strictly justified:

*"If we are made in God's image he must look curiously like an orang-outang; if we have a soul its issue must have been oddly delayed; if there is a God whose interest centres on us, what was he up to during all those billions of years before we arrived? If any arranging was done, it was we who were arranged to suit the earth and its blind environmental forces rather than vice versa; whatever might be meant by our wills being free, the way they are going to 'choose' proves astonishingly predictable from the circumstances of our lives."*

\*                    \*                    \*

Though some Christians say God is mysterious, even unknowable, there are many important things which Christians have always said they know about him. For example, he created the universe, he is all-powerful, all-knowing, just and good. Is the idea of such a God plausible?

It is not easy to believe in any being with such qualities as these. If God is all-powerful, then he could have created a world without evil, pain and disease, and he could have saved human souls without having his son nailed to a cross. Since the world obviously contains much that is bad, one has to ask whether he was unable to make a better world, or whether he did not want the world to be better. If this imperfect world was the best he could do, then his power is limited; if he did not want it to be better, then his goodness is limited.

The easy solution for anyone who wants to go on believing in God would be to sacrifice a little of his omnipotence in order to save his goodness - to say that God's power is not absolute, but limited by some other power which is evil, such as Satan.

Many peoples have believed in gods who were powerful, but not all-powerful, and for them it was possible to say that evil came not from their god, but from something that was outside their god's control. One form of this, in which the original great variety of gods was reduced not to one, but two, is known as Dualism, and it is characteristic of such religions as Zoroastrianism, which sees the cosmic process as an eternal battle between the powers of good and of evil.

The idea that evil is caused not by God but by the Devil also has a strong appeal to many Christians, such as the mediaeval Manichees and Gnostics and many of the the modern Evangelicals. But the orthodox churches, both Catholic and Protestant, have always resisted that line of thought, and those who believed that Satan was an evil power independent of God have always been condemned as heretics. The Church teaches to this day that Satan is not an independent power limiting God's omnipotence; instead, Satan was created by God and it is God's will that he exists still and works evil. Thus, God is responsible for all that Satan does.

The Church takes this line so that it can go on saying God's power is unlimited. But if nothing can limit God's power then whatever God wants must really happen. There is then a contradiction between a perfect Creator and a less than perfect creation, a contradiction that has been tormenting Christians ever since the time of the early Church: if God is perfectly good, he must want to end evil, and if he is absolutely powerful, he must be able to do so. But our experience tells us that evil has not been ended, and the world we live in is evidently not the perfect work of a perfect creator. If God sent Jesus into this world to conquer sin, he does not appear to have been altogether successful.

If God is good, why is there so much in his creation that is bad, and why does he permit badness to survive and prosper? If God is just, why does he permit so much injustice? If God loves us, why does he torture us with cruel diseases? No loving father would inflict such pain upon his children.

Professor Flew expresses the Christian believer's dilemma thus: "We cannot say that he would like to help but cannot: God is omnipotent. We cannot say that he would help if only he knew: God is omniscient. We cannot say that he is not responsible for the wickedness of others: God creates those others. Indeed, an omnipotent, omniscient God must be an accessory before (and during) the fact to every human misdeed; as well as being responsible for every non-moral defect in the universe."

John Stuart Mill once said he would rather spend eternity in hell than with the monster who sends people there.

*A whole branch of theology, known as theodicy, is dedicated to solving the problem of how God can be perfectly good in spite of the evil that is in the world. The most learned theologians in the world have been trying to solve that problem since the beginning of the Christian era. They are still trying.*

Jesus, according to the gospels, went about curing diseases. If Jesus thought that diseases were bad, and cured them in a few cases, why did he not cure all diseases, for all time? And why, if diseases were bad, did God create them or allow them in the first place?

Jesus also raised a number of people from the dead. If he thought it was a bad thing to be dead, why did he not raise all the others as well? And what happened afterwards to those he did raise? Did they die again later?

\*     \*     \*

It is often argued that there is evil in the world because God gave us free will, and so we are free to choose evil as well as good. But why did God make his creatures so bad that, given free will, we should ever wish to choose evil? If we were good, then with free will we would always wish to choose good rather than evil.

The fact that we sometimes choose evil proves that we are not the perfect creatures of a perfect God. If Adam was given free will and chose to sin, then there must have been some fault in Adam when he was made.

Anyway, most of the horrors of this world have nothing to do with men choosing evil - disease does not strike because a man chose to do evil. The dreadful suffering of the whole animal kingdom, where so many species can live only by hunting and eating others and are equipped with teeth and claws specially for that purpose, does not arise because foxes and crocodiles exercise free will and choose to do evil rather than good.

Instead of believing that the bad things in this world are a necessary consequence of free will, it is both simpler and more reasonable to believe that the order of nature was not in fact created by an all-powerful God who is just and good.

The biologist Thomas Huxley put it like this: "Since thousands of times a minute, were our ears sharp enough, we should hear sighs and groans of pain like those heard by Dante at the gate of hell, the world cannot be governed by what we call benevolence."

*Are we to believe, asked Ingersoll, that it was a God of infinite intelligence and love that made "every mouth a slaughter-house, and every stomach a tomb"?*

*In the more measured words of the philosopher Bertrand Russell: "Any omnipotent Being who created a world containing evil not due to sin must himself be at least partially evil."*

Even in human society most of the ills that we suffer do not arise because people choose to do evil. They arise by accident or by mistake, and very often because people who are trying to do good in different ways come into conflict, or else they disagree about what is the best thing to do. A great deal of harm is done by people who insist upon going about doing good.

*Evil is never due to sin among animals and seldom due to sin among humans. How, then, can all this evil be the work of a good God?*

Christians sometimes respond to this by saying that God's goodness and justice are different from ours. But in that case, why do we use our words 'good' and 'just' to describe him? If his 'goodness' is not what we would call good, and his 'justice' is sometimes what we would call unjust, then we are merely abusing our language if we choose to say that God is good and just.

A person who is able to save people from pain and disease but refuses to do it, or actually prefers to inflict the pain, will be called callous and cruel. Why, then, should a God who behaves in this way be called good and just?

It is not that God is *more* good and *more* just than we are. The problem is that his 'goodness' and 'justice' are evidently *different* from what we understand by goodness and justice. Believers may call this a mystery: we cannot understand what 'good' and 'just' mean when they are applied to God. In fact, the words have become meaningless.

Sometimes the believer will admit that God must be responsible for all the evil, pain and injustice, and then he will go on to say that these evils serve God's purpose, because good can come out of evil. But that argument overlooks God's omnipotence. If God had absolute power, then he could achieve his good purpose in another way, without the evil, pain and injustice, and if he were a good and loving father he would wish to achieve his purpose in a good and loving way, rather than by the cruel method of natural selection that we can observe in the whole of nature (a natural selection of those who can longest endure the tortures of being starved and hunted).

Could God find no other way to achieve his purpose but to make the most successful of his creatures aggressive, ferocious and carnivorous? If all this cruelty is what God intends, then he is not good, but cruel; if he cannot avoid the cruelty, then he is not omnipotent.

*　　　　*　　　　*

The atheist's question: 'If there is a God, where does evil come from?' is sometimes met by a Christian counter-question: 'If God did not exist, where do you think the good came from?'

That kind of question presupposes that good things and bad things can only exist because there is some kind of higher being which is the source of good and bad. Atheists do not believe that. They believe that the world itself is neutral; we like some things about it and dislike other things, and we invent the ideas of 'good' and 'bad' to describe what we like or dislike, but 'good' and 'bad' are not things that can exist by themselves.

*　　　　*　　　　*

As well as teaching that God is absolutely good and omnipotent, the Church also teaches that he is omniscient. He has absolute knowledge, so that he knows all things past, present and future. But this teaching also contradicts the belief in his absolute power. If he is all-knowing, so that he knows all things past, present and future, then it is impossible for the future to be otherwise than as God knows it will be. That means that he does not have the power to change it.

It also means that human beings do not have free will, since I can only do those things which God knows I am going to do. God's perfect foreknowledge cannot be wrong. (Otherwise I should have to suppose that God's omnipotence is limited by my free will. If I were free, I might decide to do something different from what God's omniscience knows I am going to do.) The same applies if God himself knows what God is going to do: he is not able to change his mind and do something else without making his own foreknowledge false. Thus, there is a logical contradiction between being omnipotent and omniscient (i.e. all-powerful and all-knowing).

We may wonder, since God is all-knowing, why believers pray to him. Do they mean to tell him something he does not already know? Do they hope that, when he has heard their prayer, God will act differently from the way he had intended to act? When they pray him to end a war or an illness, do they mean to say that they know what is the proper time to end it, that they know better than a God who is all-knowing and all-wise as well as all-powerful?

Perfect goodness, power and knowledge are only a few of the attributes which are commonly given to God. There are many more, and they also involve complications and contradictions of the same kind. Not only is there no evidence whatever that this world is governed by a being that has these attributes, but in many cases the attributes themselves are mutually contradictory.

*       *       *

As long as we are not really serious about the idea that God exists, then it is possible for us to go on describing him in vague and contradictory terms which do not pin him down in any specific way. But as soon as we take his existence seriously, we have to assume that he exists as a real being, and as such he must have certain definite characteristics and lack others. If he has any one characteristic absolutely, that makes it impossible for him also to have another characteristic which may, at some point, conflict with it.

If, as Christians say, God is a person, then he must have things which all persons have, such as a body; and a body must

85

have a definite shape, colour and sex. There is therefore some justice in those feminist jokes which challenge the old tradition that God is male (e.g. 'When God created man She was only practising') and also in their masculine counterparts (e.g. 'God was a woman until She changed Her mind'). We cannot take God seriously as a person without asking whether God is male or female, black or white, and so on. In order to *be*, one must be one thing and not another.

*We may wish to shy away from the problem by describing God in words that are vague, evasive or contradictory; but if we do that, then we have not taken his real existence seriously at all. We have merely confused the issue with a verbal smoke-screen. When words are used like that they mean nothing and therefore do not solve the problem.*

# What about faith?

We have been approaching the question of God's existence in the light of reason. We have considered the arguments, we have looked for the evidence and examined the 'proofs', and we have found that the reasons usually given for believing in God are not satisfactory. But many of those people who believe say that this is not a matter for reason. It is a matter of faith, and faith is greater than reason. Faith, not reason, gives them the strength they need to cope with the problems of this life, and it is faith, not reason, that helps them to believe.

When Kant showed that the proofs of God's existence are not valid, he said it was *necessary* for them not to work, as it left room for faith.

However, the existence of proofs or good reasons for belief would not in fact compel anyone to believe; indeed, a rational God might be pleased with those people who have faith in things which they have good reason to believe in and displeased with those who choose to ignore the evidence.

It is natural that religious people turn to their faith in times of trouble. It would be very odd if they did not. It is a great consolation for them to feel sure that their loved ones are not really dead, that everything is for the best, that God has things under control and will take care of them. It must be a very powerful comfort to feel that you are safe in the hands of a God who loves and cares for you.

In the same way, faith may help to cure diseases. If you feel sure that God will save you, that positive feeling may itself help you to get well. Just as worrying and being miserable can make you ill, so a cheerful, confident spirit can help you to conquer illness and get well again. If you are convinced that you will win, your conviction can help you win. No boxer ever predicts that he will get beaten in his next fight. Keeping your spirits up is an important part of any cure, whether it is a cure for grief, or for sickness, or for worry and despair; and a firm faith that all is well can help enormously to keep your spirits up.

*But faith works only if you really can believe in it.*

The man in the lunatic asylum who believes he is the Emperor of China may be very glad and happy that he is the Emperor of China. That belief may give him joy and comfort; if he can believe in it, then it will give him the assurance that people respect and care for him. The idea may work for him because he has faith in it. Another person, who looks at his situation in the light of reason, will not get that joy and comfort. When you consider basing your beliefs upon faith, rather than reason, then you must decide which sort of person you are: can you make yourself feel happy and secure by believing in something that is not true? Do you want to make yourself believe you are the Emperor of China so that you can feel happy?

If you can do that, you may perhaps succeed in making yourself happy. But deep down you may also be aware that your happiness is built on a lie, on self-deception, and so you will have doubts. Christian believers are often troubled by doubts and crises of faith, and they pray for help to conquer their doubts and strengthen their faith.

In the end, it is up to every individual person to decide for himself whether he wants to know how things really are, or whether he prefers to seek happiness by persuading himself to have faith. Rationalists believe that we should try to find out how things really are, and if it means facing up to some unpleasant truths, then at least by facing up to them we may stand some chance of making things better. Nothing at all will be gained if we try to persuade ourselves that a thing is true when reason tells us it is not.

Religious leaders have often been guilty of refusing to see reason and ignoring evidence which told against their case (as when they refused to look through Galileo's telescope for fear of seeing heavenly bodies which, according to Scripture, ought not to exist). Their attitude never altered the facts, but it brought discredit upon the Church.

*The great explorer Magellan once observed a lunar eclipse and noticed that the shadow of the earth was curved. He is said to have commented: "The Church says that the earth is flat. But I have seen its shadow on the moon, and I would rather trust a shadow than the Church."*

*     *     *

Christians often say that faith is not contrary to reason. But if faith were rational it would tell us to believe the same things as reason tells us to believe. There would be no problem.

If faith meant believing what it is reasonable to believe, we should not need faith. We could believe such things reasonably. We only need faith to help us believe the sort of things which it is not reasonable to believe, the sort of things which your own mind tells you are not really true. If you choose to use faith, then you are believing in spite of the evidence.

The very fact that we need faith to help us believe in God proves that reason will not lead us to that belief. The answer which reason shows us is the opposite to the answer of faith, because faith is, after all, contrary to reason. As the Bible tells us, "Faith is the substance of things hoped for, the evidence of things not seen" (Hebrews, 11,1).

The question we are asking in this book is: Does God exist? How can we approach such a question on the basis of faith, rather than reason?

Faith may have a positive value in helping people to deal with their emotions. It may help them feel confident and well, it can give them a positive attitude that helps them cope with disease or grief. It can give some people great joy and elation. But the question we have asked ourselves in this book is not a matter of emotion: it is a matter of fact. And we have absolutely no reason to suppose that believing something is true can in any way help to make it really true.

Faith may help with emotional problems; but reason is the only tool we have for evaluating and testing evidence, for weighing arguments, and so for deciding which of our ideas are likely to be true.

*Thomas Paine wrote in 1794: "The most formidable weapon against errors of every kind is reason. I have never used any other, and I trust I never shall."*

\*           \*           \*

Even Christian believers, who say we should have faith, prefer to use reason when it will help them. It is only when they reach a position where reason is against them that they say we must turn to faith. The philosopher John Locke observed that as long ago as 1689, when he wrote: "I find every sect, as far as reason will help them, make use of it gladly: and where it fails them, they cry out, It is a matter of faith, and above reason" (*Concerning Human Understanding*, Bk IV, chap. 18).

For as long as it was possible, Christians tried to prove the existence of God by logic. But now that it has become clear that those proofs do not work, most Christians do not use them any more: they find it convenient to say that the facts of religion are 'above' reason and you have to accept them by faith.

Reason is the finest tool we have for testing our beliefs and finding out the truth. Christians believe that God gave it to us. Why should God give us this power of reason if he meant us not to use it and follow where it leads, but instead to trust in faith to show us what is true?

Faith, they say, is a good thing. It is the best thing a Christian can have. According to Martin Luther and the Protestant churches, it is faith that decides whether your soul will go to heaven or to hell. If you have faith, you will be saved. Doubt is dangerous, because it might stop you believing; so you must conquer (i.e. suppress) your doubts and have faith.

When Thomas, one of the disciples of Jesus, touched Jesus's wounds to see if he had really been crucified and had risen from the dead, Jesus (according to the gospel story) reproached him and said that those people are more blessed who have believed and have not seen (John 20,24-29). So blind faith is better than clear seeing. Jesus is often angry with those who will not believe until they have seen the evidence: "Oh ye of little faith!", he says (Matthew 6,30; Luke 12,28); "Oh faithless and perverse generation, how long shall I suffer you?" (Matthew 17,17).

Christians cannot avoid saying that faith is a virtue, because they know that nobody would believe their religion if they looked at the evidence in the light of reason. They know very well that the evidence does not support their case and that reason is against them. They tried reason for as long as they thought it would help them, but by now it has become clear that it does not. So now they tell us we must have faith.

When Christians say you ought to have faith, you should try asking them: "Why must I have faith in what you tell me, rather than have faith in what somebody else tells me? Why is it good to have faith in Christianity, but not in Communism or snake-worship or flat-earthism or the Loch Ness Monster? If I ought to have faith in Jesus, shouldn't I also have faith in Jupiter or in Father Christmas?" (After all, there is fresh evidence every year for the existence of Father Christmas).

If you are going to have faith in the miracles of Jesus, should you not also have faith in the miracles of Krishna, or the miracles of Jupiter?

If it is bad to disbelieve, why do Christians disbelieve in the gods and scriptures of the Hindus?

Christians refuse to believe in many thousands of gods. Why is it bad for the atheist to disbelieve in just one more?

And if Jesus's own disciple Thomas would not believe without first seeing the evidence, why should I?

*       *       *

Faith, they say, is a virtue. Christians tell us we ought to have faith, or at least we should try to have it; they are sorry for people who lose their faith and hope they will recover it. They take for granted that faith is a good thing.

The word 'faith' is sometimes used to mean 'trust', and trust can be a good thing. I like people to trust me and life is more pleasant if they do. But trust is not always a good thing. It is not good to trust a deceiver, or to trust - instead of taking care - that things will turn out all right. Trust is not good in itself; it is a matter for our rational judgment whether we should trust a particular person or turn of events. We should not 'trust God' unless we have good reason to think he exists and is worthy of being trusted; it would hardly be a virtue to trust someone who does not exist or is not trustworthy.

We also use the word 'faith' to mean 'faithfulness', 'honesty' or 'integrity', as when we say something is done 'in good faith'. In that sense, too, faith can be a good thing (especially if the people we keep faith with are decent people rather than crooks).

These are possible meanings of the word 'faith'. But they are not what the Christian means when he is talking of his religion. When he says that God exists and the Bible is true, and he tells you to have faith, he does not mean that you should trust honest people, or be loyal to good friends, or be honest with yourself and tell the truth. He means that you should forget about your doubts and persuade yourself to believe.

The question whether God exists is a religious question. And so, whatever other meanings the word 'faith' may have, it is the religious meaning that is relevant to the question which we are discussing. And, as Richard Robinson has explained, in matters of religion the word 'faith' means "the determination to believe that there is a god no matter what the evidence may be".

*      *      *

Can it really be a virtue to have faith, rather than to apply reason to the evidence? Can it be wrong to use your own mind? Do Christians believe that God gave us a mind so that we would disbelieve and go to hell?

The French philosopher Diderot wrote a parable about this:

> *"I was lost in a great forest at night, and I had only a tiny light to guide me. A stranger came and said to me, 'My friend, put out your candle, so that you will find your way better.' That person was a theologian."*

It may be true that reason does not illuminate everything, and at times it is only a small light. But even a small light will show you more, and will show it more truly, than no light at all.

Reason will not always tell you everything that you want to know. Sometimes you have to accept that your knowledge is limited. That limitation may displease you: but you cannot get reliable knowledge by turning to faith. You could have faith in all sorts of ideas, but there is nothing except reason that can test those ideas objectively and show you which of them is more likely to be true.

Reason helps you decide which ideas are true, but faith does not. You could decide to have faith in all sorts of beliefs (e.g. those of Christianity, or Hinduism, or Communism). Faith does not tell you what to believe. It is either reason or prejudice that determines which ideas you are going to have faith in.

If you choose to have faith in irrational ideas, then reason will make you doubt those ideas, and faith will help you to suppress

93

your doubts. If your faith is not strong enough to suppress those doubts, then you will suffer what Christians call a 'crisis of faith', a crisis which they try to overcome by strengthening their faith so that they can conquer their doubts.

Conquering your reasonable doubts and having faith means believing something in spite of what your own mind is telling you. That is obviously not honest. It is lying to yourself.

*It cannot be right to lie to yourself. That is a crime against truth. And if you are an honest person you surely must want to know the truth.*

Rationalists believe you should do your best to discover the truth, taking account of whatever evidence there may be. If the evidence does not justify belief, then belief would be irrational and so it would be wrong to believe.

If you are seeking emotional strength or consolation, then it may be helpful to have faith. But if it is the truth you are after, then it is silly to suspend the judgment of your own mind and believe irrationally. As well as being silly, it is dishonest to try to believe things are true when your own mind tells you they are not.

*Therefore you should never abandon reason for the sake of faith.*

# Some modern ideas of God

In this book we have, until now, been taking the word 'God' in its traditional Christian sense - a personal God who once created the world and who still sustains and governs it. Some modern Christians have found this idea incredible; yet, rather than stop believing in God, they have tried to find new ways of defining and imagining him, ways which do not so obviously conflict with modern knowledge and offend against common sense.

The German theologian Rudolf Bultmann taught that the personal God of the Bible must be understood today as a *symbol* of the real God, who is a transcendent power: the Bible writers expressed the idea of God in human and personal terms so that people in their time could understand, but in reality God is not a super-human person, but a great world force. We must 'de-mythologise' the traditional belief - translate it into terms which are credible today.

This approach gives us a modern idea of God, but it also implies that all believers, through all the centuries, were wrong to understand God as the Bible describes him, and it is only in our time that a true understanding has, at last, been reached. That seems a trifle presumptuous. It also requires us to take a dim view of the intelligence of all Christians before us, who could not understand their own holy book, which only we have learnt to read properly.

It also seems strange that the Bible writers used language which was sure to be misunderstood through all the Christian centuries and only came to be interpreted properly in the twentieth century. They should have realised that by expressing in that way the truth, which, in Bultmann's view, they understood, they would be sure to mislead people.

Now that we have learnt at last to interpret the Bible's words as symbols, it is far from clear what the real meaning behind those symbols might be. It is difficult to understand precisely what Bultmann and his followers really mean by 'God' - to say the Bible's God is merely a symbol, and that God is not really personal, but 'transcendent' does not really tell us anything meaningful about him. The word 'God' remains, but its content has become vague.

That is even more true of another influential theologian, Paul Tillich, whose teachings were popularised in Britain by the then bishop of Woolwich, Dr John Robinson, in a famous book called *Honest to God* (1963). Tillich and his followers argue, like Bultmann, that the Bible writers described God in human and personal terms because that was most suitable for their original readers long ago. God is now to be understood as the 'Ground of our Being', the 'Depth of our Life', our 'Ultimate Concern'. Jesus, according to Tillich, is "the one in whom existence was completely transparent to essence".

So now we know, don't we?

The words that these scholars use to describe God sound impressive and mysterious (and when we write them with capital letters we can make them seem even more impressive and mysterious). But, as with Bultmann's words about his 'transcendent' and 'symbolic' God, it is not at all clear what those words really mean. The very fact that a number of different definitions all serve equally to describe God (the 'Ground of our Being', the 'Depth of our Life', our 'Ultimate Concern', the 'Depth of History', 'Hope', 'Depth') suggests that none of these phrases has any real meaning at all. They are just impressive words, and that is why they are interchangeable.

Curiously, both Tillich and Robinson recognise that it is absurd in our time to talk of God as an 'old man in the sky' in terms of 'height', which strictly means "distance outwards from the earth's surface" (Robinson, p. 12), yet both of them think it is profound to describe him in terms of 'depth'. But if a God 'up above' is no longer credible, then neither is a God 'down below'. They try to meet this problem by explaining God's 'depth' in language that does not mean 'deep' in any ordinary sense; but the very awkwardness of their explanation suggests that it does not really mean anything at all: "When Tillich speaks of God in 'depth', he is not speaking of another Being *at all*. He is speaking of 'the infinite and inexhaustible depth and ground of all being', of our ultimate concern, of what we take seriously without reservation" (Robinson, p. 46). Do words like these describe a God who really exists, a God in whom we could believe and to whom it would make sense to address our prayers?

By re-defining the word 'God' to mean 'Ultimate Reality', Tillich and Robinson tried to make it appear ridiculous not to believe in God. Even atheists would find it hard to say that ultimate reality does not exist. But 'ultimate reality' is not what the word 'God' has meant to believers through all the ages, and it is arbitrary to decide that this is what it ought to mean now. 'Ultimate reality' is in any case not the clearest of ideas, and it seems to imply that ordinary reality is in some way not quite real. These theologians have not made it more credible that God exists; what they have done is to re-define the word 'God' until it suggests something so vague and incoherent that nobody can say whether it exists or not.

These new and mysterious ideas of God are, in fact, no more satisfactory than the old traditional idea of God as a superhuman person, as he is described in the Bible. They represent what the British theologian John Hick has called Christianity's attempt "to adapt itself into something which can be believed". But when the incredible features of Christianity's God are stripped away, nothing remains that has any real meaning. We are left with mysterious, but empty words.

Professor G. A. Wells, in his book *Religious Postures* (1988), describes very clearly the efforts made by modern theologians to adapt their religious beliefs into "something which can be believed". We may respect and admire these theologians for daring to question the traditional view and for facing up to real objections against their God which other believers preferred to ignore; but we cannot say that they have solved the problem of making God's existence more credible.

*       *       *

An idea that has now been generally abandoned by theologians but still has a popular appeal is that God has revealed himself to mankind in a progressive way, inspiring the early Jews with a vision of himself which suited their culture and understanding, but giving later generations more advanced knowledge, so that the truth has been gradually unfolded as man has become better able to understand.

This explanation seemed attractive at the beginning of the present century, but we hear little of it from theologians today: perhaps that is because, on closer inspection, it has been found not to serve their purpose.

The Christian teacher who wishes to use this theory must begin by discarding his own Bible. It is now some two thousand years old and so it represents a view of God and the world which may perhaps have suited the Jews of antiquity but has by now become outgrown and superseded. And, unfortunately for the theory, our modern understanding has been revealed to us not through pious priests and churchmen who were inspired by God, but mainly through secular scientists, most of whom no longer believe in him. God moves in a mysterious way, his wonders to perform.

When truth is gradually unfolded we expect even the early stages to be true. Later revelations will then give a fuller picture. But the world view of Genesis is patently ridiculous and that of the gospels (where diseases are caused because the body is inhabited by evil spirits) is hardly an advance. Similarly with the moral teachings: it is hard to see how the brutal savagery recommended by God in the first books of the Bible could

98

possibly be a useful first step towards anything that is good and humane. When we move onwards and upwards from this savagery to the teachings of the Christian gospels and the holy Fathers, we learn that I will be burned for ever in hell for writing this book and you will suffer the same torments if you agree with me. Is that moral progress?

*It may be wise, in educating children, not to give them the whole truth at once; but the early lessons should at least be true and dependable, a sound foundation for what is to come, and we do not expect the various steps of the revelation to contradict each other.*

Theological study itself has shown, especially in the present century, that almost everything in the Jewish and Christian scriptures appears also in the traditions of other ancient peoples, and in many cases the non-Christian traditions are older. Other nations who were neighbours of the ancient Israelites had their own creation myths, stories of a flood, god-given codes of laws and morals, their prophets and holy men and tales of gods who died and were resurrected: we can see how the Jewish and Christian traditions arose out of beliefs that were already current among their neighbours at the time. That makes it hard for us to believe that these ideas were revealed to the Jews and Christians by God himself.

If the Jewish and Christian religions were stages of God's revelation to mankind, we would expect them to be ahead of the thinking of other people. But the teachings of such people as Confucius, Pythagoras, Socrates and Aristotle are clearly more advanced, both in science and morality, than those of the first Christians who lived many centuries later. Four hundred years before Jesus, the Greek Hippocrates had been founding the scientific study of medicine on the belief that "every illness has a natural cause"; but in the Christian gospels the cause is an evil spirit and there is no cure unless God performs a miracle. Is that a 'progressive revelation'?

In science, as in morality, it is hard to see what God revealed to the Christians that was not already well known to others long before.

Today, at the latest stage of God's revelation, which should, according to the theory, be the most advanced, we still see many different religions conflicting with each other, indeed still at war with each other in several parts of the world. There is not much evidence that the followers of those religions are any wiser or more enlightened than those of us who reject their kind of wisdom and enlightenment and who expect the truth to be found by careful observation and reasoning, rather than given to us by any divine revelation.

*As Ingersoll wrote: "No god ever was in advance of the nation that created him."*

# Conclusion

We have examined the reasons which are generally advanced for believing in the existence of God and found them to be faulty; and we have not found any other reason. For the rationalist the only conclusion is that he cannot justify the belief that God exists.

I do not pretend to have proved that God does not exist. Non-existence is not a thing that can be proven. But I do claim that the arguments produced by believers are not sufficient to justify their belief. It is possible that this world contains gods and fairies, flying pigs and the Holy Spirit: nobody can prove they do not exist. But it is sensible not to believe in such things until those who say they exist have produced such evidence as will make it more reasonable for us to believe than not to believe.

In the case of the traditional Christian God the disbeliever's position is even stronger, because traditional belief contains many absurdities and contradictions which make it logically impossible. The kind of God in whom Christians used to believe is therefore demonstrably false. And while the traditional God has become incredible, the attempts of some modern theologians to redefine God as "something which can be believed" have failed to produce anything more than impressive but meaning-less words. Thus, we have to give up the old kind of God but have no reason for believing in any other kind.

\*        \*        \*

Since it is not possible either to prove or to disprove God's existence conclusively, some people adopt an agnostic position. The agnostic believes that we have insufficient evidence and must therefore leave the question open. But, since the question is important and affects the way we live our lives, it is hard in practice to make no decision: in fact, most agnostics live their lives as though God did not exist. If that is what they really believe, then they are using the word 'agnostic' as a polite euphemism so as to avoid declaring themselves atheists. It seems to me that, after considering the arguments for the hypothesis that God exists, we have more reason for disbelief than for declaring ourselves unable to decide. The atheist's position is therefore the more reasonable.

Nobody can compel you to be reasonable: you may prefer to have faith. That is up to you. Faith is a personal matter. But reason has important advantages. For one thing, it enables you to choose, and to choose justly, whereas faith is itself believing and cannot help you decide which beliefs to have faith in. To make that decision you have to use either reason or prejudice.

If you choose to approach the question rationally - that is, if you look for the evidence and examine it, if you check the arguments advanced by those who believe and consider whether they are valid - then, I believe, you will find those arguments wholly inadequate to support their case.

Some people will choose to believe what they wish to believe, regardless of any evidence or argument. But for the rationalist the idea of 'God' is an unnecessary hypothesis, and hypotheses are not to be multiplied beyond necessity.

*There is therefore no good reason to believe in the existence of God.*

*     *     *

It will be objected that this conclusion is negative. Atheists are very often accused of being negative, and it is regarded as a fault. But to this the atheist can fairly reply that all of us are negative towards the things which we regard as bad: doctors are negative towards diseases, teachers take a negative view of ignorance and the religious believer is negative about atheism.

To believe in a world without gods is not really any more negative than to believe in one that includes gods. It is simply to understand the world differently.

Whether a point of view appears negative or positive depends mainly upon the form of words in which it is expressed. Thomas Paine rejected both the fervent English nationalism and the Christian religion of his time, but he expressed his rejection of these things in very positive words which I, for one, would still commend today:

*"My country is the world, and my religion is to do good."*

# Notes

Page 3    Today the Church punishes suicide by refusing the body a normal burial in consecrated ground. A common mediaeval punishment, which survived in Catholic France to the late 18th century, was to be dragged naked through the streets and then publicly hanged.

Page 3    The ritual slaughter of meat was severely criticised in a report by the Farm Animals Welfare Council in 1985; it is also opposed by the RSPCA and the British Veterinary Council. But it still continues, and halal meat is often sold in ordinary shops where the customer may be unaware of the method of slaughter that was used.

Page 6    The words I have quoted from the Oxford English Dictionary are the first and general definition of 'god'. It is followed by other definitions which apply when the word is used in some narrower special sense.

Page 9    The belief that the stars and planets were gods was undermined when Thales of Miletus, in the sixth century BC, learned from Babylonian sources how to predict their movements (see James Thrower, *A History of Western Atheism*, London 1971, p. 11). Thales correctly predicted the solar eclipse of 585 BC. Anaxagoras later denied the divinity of first the moon, then the other celestial bodies.

Page 10    Pythagoras first speculated that the earth goes round the sun, and not the sun round the earth, in the 6th century BC. When Copernicus two thousand years later found evidence to prove that this is correct, he kept his book secret for 36 years, until his death in 1543. It was then published, and the Inquisition condemned it at once as "that false Pythagorean doctrine utterly contrary to the Holy Scriptures". They declared Copernicus a heretic and placed his work on the *Index of Forbidden Books*. Not long afterwards, the work of Galileo showed that Copernicus had been right; Galileo was then forced to recant and to swear that the sun, and not the earth, was moving. In spite of recanting he was imprisoned and when he died the Church would not allow the burial of his body in consecrated ground. The philosopher Giordano Bruno said that distant stars were like the sun, with inhabited planets circling round them. For this he was burned at the stake in Rome in 1600.

Page 11   Nicolas Walter's book *Blasphemy Ancient and Modern*, (Rationalist Press Association, London 1990), quotes numerous examples
of the suppression of free thought and shows that suppression of
dissent is the usual policy in religious societies (thus, p. 9: "it seems
that in most places and at most times any open challenge to
prevailing religious beliefs has been suppressed by force. In particular, all established religions which have possessed political
power have persecuted blasphemy, and none more so than the
powerful monotheistic religions of Judaism, Christianity and Islam"). Nearly all Christian teachers agreed that heresy (holding a
false religious opinion) should be punished by death, and the death
penalty was in fact imposed for over a thousand years in Christian
Europe (see pp. 17-18).

Page 13   Florence Nightingale believed in God, but not in the personal God
of Christianity. Her idea of 'God' was that of the Deists, like
Voltaire and Thomas Paine. She thought it selfish of Christians to
be so concerned about their own salvation, and she regarded Jesus
Christ as a man who had been seriously wrong about the nature of
God and the rôle of mankind. She rejected the moral teaching of
Jesus as being too passive and negative. Since Christian writers
sometimes quote her work as an example of the Christian religion
in action it is salutary to read Margaret Knight's study of this
subject, "Florence Nightingale's religion", in *Question*, vol. 10
(1977), pp. 52-58.

Page 13   The psalmist of the Old Testament complains "The fool hath said
in his heart, There is no God" (Psalm 14,1; also 53,1). So even
among the ancient Israelites there were disbelievers.

Page 15   To quote Bradlaugh: "Every child is born into the world an Atheist,
and, if he grows into a Theist, his Deity differs with the country in
which the believer may happen to be educated. The belief is the
result of education or organization." (from his essay 'A Plea for
Atheism', written in the late 1870s). It is also true that when people
'experience' God's presence, the God they experience is always
the one of their own particular culture and environment. Christians
are not visited by Krishna or Vishnu, nor Hindus by Christ.

Page 16   "A wise man ... proportions his belief to the evidence", David
Hume, *An Enquiry Concerning Human Understanding* (1748),
section 10 ('Of Miracles'), I,86.

105

Page 17    The First Vatican Council in 1870 made it a dogma of the Church that God "can be known through creation by the natural light of human reason" and that anyone who denies this shall be anathema, i.e. cast out of the Church (see Flew, *God and Philosophy*, p.12). It is therefore necessary for all Roman Catholics to believe that the existence and nature of God can be proven by reasoning.

Page 18    The Ambrosian hymn is *Deus creator omnium*.

Page 19    St Thomas Aquinas argues (*Summa Theol.* I, q.2, a.3): "Whatever lacks knowledge cannot move towards an end, unless it be directed by some being endowed with knowledge and intelligence, as the arrow is directed by the archer. Therefore some intelligent being exists by whom all natural things are ordered to their end; and this being we call God."

Page 19    The philosophy of St Thomas Aquinas was declared the official philosophy of the Roman Catholic Church by Pope Leo XIII in 1879 and reaffirmed in the encyclical *Humani Generis* in 1950.

Page 20    The classical Roman writer Cicero declared: "The celestial order and the beauty of the universe compel me to admit that there is some excellent and eternal Being who deserves the respect and homage of men" (*De Divinitatione*, II,72, 148).

Page 20    Pantheists are those whose 'God' is nature itself, Deists are those who use the hypothesis of God to explain the beginning of the universe, which God created and set into motion, since which he has done nothing at all.

Page 21    Jeremy Bentham parodied the idea that God laid down the 'laws' of nature by describing thus how it happened (taking as his example the laws of optics): "Hark ye (said the author of nature once upon a time), hark ye, you rays. There are some surfaces which you will meet with in your travels that when you strike upon them, will send you packing; now when in such case, this is what I would have you do: keep the same slope in *going* that you did in coming. Mind and do what I say: if you don't, as sure as you are rays it will be the worse for you: upon this the rays (finding they should get into bad bread else) made their bows, shrugged up their shoulders and went and did so." (J. Bentham, *A Comment on the Commentaries*, ed. C. W. Everett, London 1928, p. 32).

Page 22    At the end of chapter 7 of his *Dialogues Concerning Natural Religion* Hume observes that the spider does not design her web and asks "why an orderly system may not be spun from the belly as well as from the brain".

Page 23    Paley's statement of the 'Argument from Design' appears at the beginning of the first chapter of his *Natural Theology* (London 1802), which opens thus: "In crossing a heath, suppose I pitched my foot against a *stone*, and were asked how the stone came to be there: I might possibly answer, that, for any thing I knew to the contrary, it had lain there for ever; nor would it perhaps be very easy to show the absurdity of this answer. But suppose I had found a *watch* upon the ground, and it should be inquired how the watch happened to be in that place; I should hardly think of the answer which I had before given, - that, for any thing I knew, the watch might have always been there. Yet why should not this answer serve for the watch as well as for the stone? Why is it not as admissible in the second case, as in the first? For this reason, and for no other, viz. that, when we come to inspect the watch, we perceive (what we could not discover in the stone) that its several parts are framed and put together for a purpose . . ."

Page 24    The 'creation' of new particles of matter (and antimatter) out of energy, which sometimes happens in atomic physics, is not making something out of nothing: it is converting something from one form into another. If you are interested in this, read Paul Davies, *God and the New Physics* (Penguin Books, 1984), pp. 25-32.

Page 27    Some critics have objected that Darwin's 'survival of the fittest' is really a tautology, because 'fitness' is proved by the actual fact of survival. Thus, those who survive survive. But this can only be done if we misrepresent Darwin's theory. The 'fittest' are not simply those who happen to survive, but those who have features which are found to promote survival. It is not the case that animals survive at random and may then be called 'the fittest'; instead, we observe that individuals with certain qualities are more likely to survive, and these may be called 'the fittest'. Though the fittest individual may not survive, the advantage ensures that their kind will prevail statistically. On this see A. Flew, *A Rational Animal and other Philosophical Essays about the Nature of Man*, Oxford 1978, chapter 1, 'The Darwinian Framework', pp. 12-14.

Page 30    W. K. Clifford is quoted by Annie Besant in her article 'Why I Do Not Believe in God', reprinted in Stein's *Anthology of Atheism and Rationalism* (Prometheus Books), Buffalo 1980, p. 30.

Page 34 "Since everything was made for a purpose, it follows that every-thing is made for the best purpose. Observe: our noses were made to carry spectacles, so we have spectacles. Legs were clearly intended for breeches, and we wear them ... And since pigs were made to be eaten, we eat pork all the year round." Voltaire, *Candide*, chapter 1.

Page 35 The restatement of the ontological proof which I quote is that of Hector Hawton in his *Men Without Gods* (Thinker's Library), London 1948, p. 54.

Page 36 St Anselm (1033-1109) in his formulation of the 'proof' defines God as "something than which nothing greater can be conceived" (*"aliquid quo nihil maius cogitari possit"*). A being that exists not only in the mind, but also in reality is greater than one that exists in the mind alone. Therefore the greatest being we can conceive exists in both. Anselm argued later that God's existence is logically necessary, and a necessary existence is greater than a 'contingent' existence (one that is factual, but not necessary). Descartes (1596-1650) reformulated the argument, saying that a "supremely perfect being" cannot be deficient in existence, which is necessary to perfection. Both forms were demolished by Kant (1724-1804). A number of attempts have been made since Kant's time to reformu-late the argument so as to avoid the objections, but none has proved successful.

Page 36 The 'ontological proof' presupposes that existence is more perfect than non-existence. But that is not self-evident and there are some people, such as Buddhists, who would not agree.

Page 37 St Bernard's 'solution' appears in his interpretation of Psalm 85,10: "Mercy and truth are met together; righteousness and peace have kissed each other."

Page 37 As Young says in his *Night Thoughts*: "A God all mercy is a God unjust" (Night 4, 234).

Page 38 The actual example given by Professor Moore is quoted in Antony Flew's *God and Philosophy*, London 1966, p. 80: "with other grammatically appropriate terms you can significantly if not truly say that some tame tigers do it and some do not. But it makes no sense at all to say that some tame tigers exist, and some do not (Moore)."

Page 38    There is another difficulty about the ontological proof. If it is true
           that the most perfect being imaginable must have the 'attribute' of
           existence, then the least perfect being imaginable must be without
           that 'attribute'. Any imperfect being, having existence, would be
           even more imperfect deprived of existence. So if the ontological
           proof really did prove the existence of God, it would at the same
           time also prove the non-existence of the most imperfect being
           imaginable, whom Christians call the Devil.

Page 41    St Augustine tried to deal with the problem of God changing his
           mind when he decided to create the universe, after having rested for
           an infinite time without wanting to create one. He said that God
           does not exist in time, but in eternity. Thus, God created the world
           "at no time" (he argues thus in his *Confessions*, book 11). The
           problem for us is, as usual: does this mean anything? Is there really
           something called 'eternity' which is different from time, and not
           just an infinite period of time? Or is it merely a play upon words
           to talk of things happening 'outside of time'? Can time really have
           a beginning? If you imagine a beginning of time, when God created
           time, could you not imagine ten minutes before that beginning
           (even though there was no clock to measure those ten minutes)?

Page 41    Bradlaugh's remark, which concludes his argument against the
           'First Cause' theory, will be found in his essay 'A Plea for
           Atheism', which was written in the late 1870s and may be found
           in *Humanity's Gain from Unbelief*, a collection of his writings
           published in the Thinker's Library in 1929, p. 46.

Page 42    In the 18th century David Hume questioned the assumption that
           every event must have a cause. He argued that causation applies
           when we regularly see one event follow another and so we predict
           that the second event will also in future follow the first. But this
           prediction is possible only in cases where both events have often
           been observed. It could not apply to creation unless we had often
           seen worlds created and observed that creation always follows an
           act of God.

Page 43    Kant's argument that we must believe in God in order to validate
           our moral behaviour will be found in his *Critique of Pure Reason*,
           Part Two, chapter 2, section 2. What it comes to is that our moral
           behaviour would be irrational if God did not exist. Since Kant does
           not show that moral behaviour is rational, this argument does
           nothing to make God's real existence more likely.

Page 44    Margaret Knight, in her book *Honest to Man* (pp. 6-7), deals lucidly with the argument that 'good' is derived from God. She also gives, in the following pages, examples of morality in non-human animals which live in groups, especially baboons, showing that morality arises in any society, human or animal, because the survival of any society depends upon co-operation between its members and control of the selfish instincts of individuals.

Page 46    The poem on the rain's indifference to moral values is by Charles Bowen (1835-94). Its biblical inspiration is the gospel of St Matthew, chapter 5, verse 45: "He maketh his sun to rise on the evil and on the good, and sendeth rain on the just and on the unjust."

Page 46    In AD 524 the great Roman statesman and thinker Boethius wrote: "It may be part of human weakness to have evil wishes, but it is nothing short of monstrous that God should look on while every criminal is allowed to achieve his purpose against the innocent." (*The Consolation of Philosophy*, book 1, chapter 4).

Page 46    Aristotle wrote in Book I of his *Politics*: "Man is by nature a social animal".

Page 48    Ingersoll's remark will be found in the first paragraph of his article "Some Mistakes of Moses", reprinted in Stein's *Anthology of Atheism and Rationalism*, p. 146.

Page 49    St Bernard wrote in his *De Laude Novae Militiae, Caput iii* ('De Militibus Christi') that the crusader, when he kills an unbeliever, is not *homicida* but *malicida*, avenging Christ against the evil-doer (Migne, *Patrologia, series Latina*, vol. 182, c. 924).

Page 53    Sir Hermann Bondi's example is taken from a radio talk entitled "Why I don't like religion", broadcast on BBC Radio 4 on 5th October 1976 and published in the *New Humanist*, vol. 93, no. 2 (September 1977), pp. 83-84.

Page 56    The story about the gardener will be found in Professor Flew's essay "Theology and Falsification", first published in 1950 and reprinted in *The Presumption of Atheism*, p. 72 (also in Margaret Knight's *Humanist Anthology*, pp. 192-4). It first appeared, in a different and longer form, in John Wisdom's article "Gods", in the *Proceedings of the Aristotelian Society,* London 1944-5.

Page 61    I refer to the Religious Experience Research Unit, set up at Oxford University in 1969 by Professor Sir Alister Hardy.

Page 63    Einstein's criticism of the 'God of the gaps' will be found in his *Ideas and Opinions,* translated by S. Bargmann, London 1973, p. 48.

Page 67    Sir Karl Popper, to whom we owe the modern theory of scientific method, has taught us that all theories must live dangerously: they have to be exposed to criticism and their supporters must be willing to admit evidence that might prove they are wrong. We can never know for certain that any hypothesis is true, but we can know that a hypothesis is false. If I believe that all swans are white, I cannot prove my hypothesis by observing a hundred or a million white swans; but if I observe one black swan then I know for certain that the hypothesis is false. Therefore a hypothesis must be tested not by quoting cases which agree with it but by seeking evidence that would 'falsify' it, and the person who puts forward a hypothesis must be prepared to specify what will happen if his theory is true and what sort of evidence would convince him that he is wrong.

Page 68    The quotation is from Winwood Reade's *The Martyrdom of Man*; this book, first published in 1872, is still a fascinating and instructive account of the origin of human civilisation.

Page 68    J. M. Robertson comments thus on early man's assumption that all natural things are alive: "A dog, seeing an open umbrella moved along the ground by the wind, will show that he regards it as a living thing. To his ignorance, it may very well be so. To the ignorance of the savage, there may be a will and personality in the blowing of the wind and in the rising of the flood, as there is in the only purposive actions of which he knows anything - those of men and animals. On the basis of natural ignorant guessing, religious systems slowly arise." ('Godism' in Stein's *Anthology of Atheism and Rationalism,* p. 72.)

Page 69    "So God created man in his own image, in the image of God created he him"(*Genesis* 1,27). On that verse Voltaire commented: "If God created us in his own image we have more than reciprocated" (*Le Sottisier*).

Page 69    The quotation from Xenophanes is from Fragment 15. Russell's observation will be found in his *Unpopular Essays,* p. 85, and Montesquieu's in his *Lettres persanes,* 59.

Page 69    Rupert Brooke's poem, from which I have quoted only a few lines, is entitled 'Heaven'. It is quoted in full, together with other poems of interest to humanists, in Bet Cherrington's anthology *Facing the World*, published by Pemberton, London 1989.

Page 70   God's reason for performing his miracles, according to the New Testament, is usually to convince disbelievers. Yet in past ages, when almost everyone believed, there were plenty of miracles, while today, when there are many disbelievers, they do not appear.

Page 71   Hume's essay "On Miracles" is a classic of philosophy and well worth reading. It is section 10 of his *An Inquiry Concerning Human Understanding*, first published in 1748.

Page 71   "Is it more probable that nature should go out of her course, or that a man should tell a lie?", Thomas Paine, *The Age of Reason*, p. 66.

Page 72   Spinoza pointed out (*Ethics*, Pt. I, appendix) that if God has a purpose, then he now lacks something which he seeks to achieve. But if he lacks something he is not perfect.

Page 75   A full report on delinquency among Catholics is given by Nicolas Walter in the *New Humanist*, vol. 94 (1978), no. 1, p. 5, and no. 2, pp. 44-45; the figures for Britain are from the *Report on the Work of the Prison Department*, 1978, and they agree with a number of earlier surveys which are also quoted. Similar results have been found from surveys conducted in Australia, New Zealand, the United States and the Netherlands, see Michael Argyle, *Religious Behaviour* (1958) and Antony Flew, "Against Indoctrination", in *The Humanist Outlook*, ed. by A. J. Ayer (1968).

Page 76   The papal encyclical *Caritate Christi Compulsi* urges the poor to endure their sufferings because those sufferings are part of God's plan: "Let the poor, and all those who at this time are facing the hard trial of want of work and security of food - let them in a like spirit of penance suffer with greater resignation the privations imposed upon them by these hard times and the state of the society which Divine Providence, in an inscrutable but ever-loving plan, has assigned to them", quoted by Hector Hawton, *Controversy: The Humanist/Christian Encounter*, (Pemberton) London 1971, p. 57.

Page 79   I quote Alex Carey from his article "The Scientific Attitude", in Ian Edwards, *A Humanist View*, Sydney 1969, p. 26.

Page 80   Zoroastrianism is the religion of the Parsees (in Persia). It teaches that good was created by Ormuzd, God of Light, and evil by Ahriman, the God of Darkness, and the universe is a battle ground between Ormuzd with his angels and Ahriman with his devils. This religion had a strong effect on Christian heresies.

Page 81 Professor Flew is quoted from his *New Essays in Philosophical Theology* (SCM Press), London 1963, p. 107.

Page 82 "Would an infinitely wise, good and powerful God, intending to produce man, commence with the lowest possible forms of life ... and, during immeasurable periods of time, slowly and almost imperceptibly improve upon the rude beginning, until man was evolved? Would countless ages thus be wasted in the production of awkward forms, afterwards abandoned? Can the intelligence of man discover the least wisdom in covering the earth with crawling, creeping horrors that live only upon the agonies and pangs of others? Can we see the propriety of so constructing the earth, that only an insignificant portion of its surface is capable of producing an intelligent man? Who can appreciate the mercy of so making the world that all animals devour animals; so that every mouth is a slaughter-house, and every stomach a tomb? Is it possible to discover infinite intelligence and love in universal and eternal carnage?" Ingersoll, *Oration on the Gods*, p. 33.

Page 84 John Hick, in his book *Evil and the God of Love* (p.11), explains very fairly that the non-believer does not need to answer the question 'where did good come from?' because he accepts the universe as given and finds it partly pleasant and partly unpleasant. He does not have to assume that the pleasant things were made by a good power and the unpleasant things by an evil power: "It is the Christian theist who claims that the situation is other than it appears, in that there is an invisible divine Being who is perfect in goodness and unlimited in power. And the problem of evil arises at this point as a genuine difficulty that he is bound to face. Si deus est, unde malum?"

Page 85 The problem that God's omniscience prevents me from having free will was considered by St Thomas Aquinas, the great mediaeval philosopher whose definitions of Christian faith and doctrine came to be accepted by the Catholic Church. He argued thus: "At the height of eternity God regards all things from above the movement of time. When I see Socrates sitting down, my knowledge is certain and infallible, but it imposes no necessity on Socrates to sit. And so God, in looking at things which are to us past, present or future, infallibly and certainly knows them as present realities, yet without imposing on them the necessity of existing." (*Opusculum* 26, 'De Rationibus Fidei ad Cantorem Antiochenum', 10). This argument is really an echo of St Augustine, who had said long before: "God does not foresee the future - he sees it."

Once again the great Christian teachers deceive us by their dexterity with words: in this case it is the unclearness of the word 'eternity' that baffles us, so that we might easily overlook the real difference that time makes. There is a big difference between watching what I do now and watching what I am going to do tomorrow. If you watch me sitting down now, your knowledge does not interfere with my free will: I could, if I wanted to, stand on my head instead of sitting down. Then you would have certain knowledge of my standing on my head. As long as you watch me in the present time, your watching does not stop me from doing whatever I like. My doing determines what you must see.

But if anybody, even God, watches me doing what I am going to do tomorrow, then what I am going to do is now fixed. I may not know myself what I am going to do, but as long as anyone has certain knowledge of it, it cannot be otherwise, and it is not possible for me to do something different. His seeing will have determined what I must do.

What matters is not whether God's knowledge is called 'seeing' or 'foreseeing'; it makes no difference whether he 'sees' from the height of eternity or 'foresees' like a fortune-teller. The important thing is whether he knows the present or the future. If he knows certainly and infallibly what I am going to do, then I cannot be free not to do it.

Page 91  Two great rationalists, Thomas Paine and Thomas Huxley, both said that Doubting Thomas was their patron saint.

Page 92  J. M. Robertson wrote in his essay "Godism" (about 1896, quoted in Stein's *Anthology of Atheism and Rationalism*, p. 74): "*You* deny the existence of nine-hundred-and-ninety-nine alleged Gods. *I* merely deny one more - yours."

Page 93  The definition of faith, as the word is used in religious contexts, is quoted from Richard Robinson, *An Atheist's Values*, p. 120.

Page 93  Diderot's parable will be found in his *Pensées sur la religion*, first published anonymously in 1763 but openly attributed to Diderot after his death. They appeared in English in the *New Humanist*, vol. 98 (Winter 1982), pp. 13-15.

114

Page 96    "The word 'God' denotes the ultimate depth of all our being, the creative ground and meaning of all our existence" (Robinson, *Honest to God,* p. 47).

Page 100   Ingersoll's words will be found in his *Oration on the Gods*, p. 11.

# Suggestions for further reading

Richard Dawkins, *The Blind Watchmaker* (1987)

Antony Flew, *God and Philosophy* (1966)

Antony Flew, *The Presumption of Atheism* (1976), reprinted as *God, Freedom and Immortality : A Critical Analysis* (1984)

Michael Goulder and John Hick, *Why Believe in God?* (SCM Press, 1983)

Hector Hawton, *Controversy: The Humanist/Christian Encounter* (1971)

John Hick, *Arguments for the Existence of God* (Macmillan), London 1970

David Hume, *Dialogues Concerning Natural Religion*, London 1779

David Hume, *Of Miracles* (= section 10 of *An Enquiry Concerning Human Understanding*, 1748)

Margaret Knight, *A Humanist Anthology* (1961)

Margaret Knight, *Honest to Man* (1974)

Thomas Paine, *The Age of Reason* (1794)

William Paley, *Natural Theology; or, Evidences of the existence and attributes of the deity, collected from the appearances of nature* (1802)

Winwood Reade, *The Martyrdom of Man* (1872)

John Robinson, *Honest to God* (SCM), London 1963

Richard Robinson, *An Atheist's Values* (Blackwell), Oxford 1964

Bertrand Russell, *Unpopular Essays* (Allen and Unwin), London 1950

Bertrand Russell, *Why I am not a Christian* (1927, reprinted together with *The Faith of a Rationalist*, 1947, as an R.P.A. booklet, 1983)

George H. Smith, *The Case Against God* (Prometheus) Buffalo 1979

Gordon Stein, *An Anthology of Atheism and Rationalism* (Prometheus) Buffalo 1980)

G. A. Wells, *Did Jesus Exist?* (1975, second ed. 1986)

G. A. Wells, *Religious Postures* (Open Court), La Salle 1988

Some of these books (e.g. Hume, Paine, Paley) are well known classics. Goulder and Hick is obtainable from the SCM Press. Most of the others, and a list of further literature and prices, may be obtained from the Rationalist Press Association, 88 Islington High Street, London N1 8EW.